lisa ? (handwritten)

NOT EXTINCT

Keeping the Sinixt Way

MARILYN JAMES & TARESS ALEXIS
with the Blood of Life Collective

Maa Press, New Denver, BC

© MAA PRESS 2018

Published by Maa Press
P.O. Box 69
New Denver, BC, V0G 1S0
www.maapress.ca
info@maapress.ca

Design and Production: Amélie Blanchard, a freelance graphic designer and visual artist. She can be contacted at ameliecblanchard@gmail.com for future projects.

Printed in Canada by Houghton Boston Printers on FSC® certified paper

The stories, which form the backbone of this book, are available for free download by those who purchase this book, or on CD, at www.maapress.ca. The username to download the audio files is : senk'lip and the password is: tum xula7xw

Library and Archives Canada Cataloguing in Publication
James, Marilyn, 1952-, author
        Not extinct : keeping the Sinixt way / by Marilyn James
and Taress Alexis ; with the Blood of Life Collective.

Includes bibliographical references and index.
ISBN 978-0-9685302-8-3 (softcover)

1. Sinixt Indians--British Columbia. I. Alexis, Taress, 1981-, author II. Title.

E99.S546J36 2018   971.1004'979   C2017-907595-0

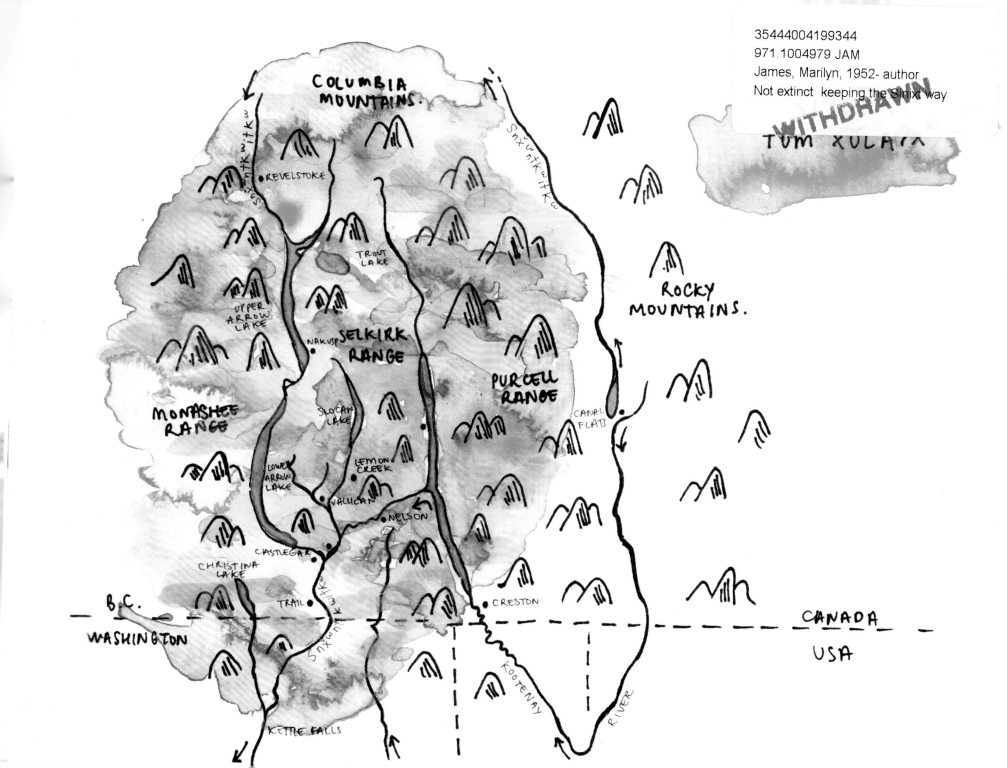

TUM XULA?X

COLUMBIA
MOUNTAINS.

snx̌ʷntkʷitkʷ

REVELSTOKE

snx̌ʷntkʷitkʷ

ROCKY
MOUNTAINS.

TROUT
LAKE

UPPER
ARROW
LAKE

SELKIRK
RANGE

NAKUSP

PURCELL
RANGE

MONASHEE
RANGE

SLOCAN
LAKE

CANAL
FLATS

LEMON
CREEK

LOWER
ARROW
LAKE

VALLICAN

NELSON

CASTLEGAR

CHRISTINA
LAKE

snx̌ʷntkʷus

TRAIL

CRESTON

CANADA

B.C.

WASHINGTON

USA

KOOTENAY

RIVER

KETTLE FALLS

TABLE OF CONTENTS

ACKNOWLEDGMENTS

We would like to acknowledge and say *lim limpt* to our elders and ancestors who shared these stories and kept them alive. We acknowledge and lift our hands to Mourning Dove and her publication of *Coyote Stories* (University of Nebraska Press reprint, Mourning Dove's Coyote Stories [1990]). We would also like to acknowledge that the Takwiya story is not a Sinixt story. It is a Coastal Salish story and we are grateful to have had it shared with us and to be able to share it as an aspect of inter-cultural sharing of knowledge and creation. These stories are not ours – they belong to all the people. We are merely upholding our responsibility to share them and thus keep them alive. Some of these stories have been told in different ways; we acknowledge and accept our creative licence and own any fault if someone takes exception to our version. All personal experiences and opinions depicted are our own and we accept them as such.

We'd also like to acknowledge Ted Moomaw for providing essential information on meaning and spelling of Sinixt words, phrases and terms. However, as the written language is still evolving, we take full responsibility for any issues people may find with spelling or usage.

Without the support of the Nelson and District Women's Centre, especially Lisa McGreary, and Kootenay Co-operative Radio's ongoing backing, this project could never have come to fruition. Deep thanks for your time and care. Thank you to Joe Hetherington for essential financial and personal support in helping this book emerge. Gratitude to Julian Ross (of Polestar Calendars) and Ginger Mason for emotional and practical support in the publishing process.

The creative development of this far-ranging project has been funded through: Grants to Aboriginal Peoples of the Canada Council for the Arts, the Columbia Kootenay Cultural Alliance of the Columbia Basin Trust and the British Columbia Arts Council.

INTRODUCTION
Marilyn James

Sinixt *tum xúlaʔxᵂ*, our traditional territory, takes in a huge landscape area. It takes in the Columbia Mountains to the north which are above Revelstoke. That mountain mass is billions of years old. That's the birthplace of the Columbia Mountains. Spilling out of that range to the West of the Sinixt *tum xúlaʔxᵂ* would be the height of the Monashee mountain range which goes down from Revelstoke west of the Arrow Lakes Reservoir and then goes off toward Rock Creek and Osoyoos. That's the Monashee. To the East it would have taken in the Rocky Mountains east of Revelstoke and have gone south. But those were the traditional days of the *tum xúlaʔxᵂ*. In contemporary times, the *tum xúlaʔxᵂ* goes from the height of the Purcells, taking in the Selkirks, going west to the height of the Monashees. The *tum xúlaʔxᵂ* goes down below the US-Canadian border, 80% of the territory being north of the US-Canadian border and 20% being below the US-Canadian border. (Note: a glossary of Sinixt words and their approximate pronunciation is at the back of the book.)

The stories of this book are the stories that depict the *captikᵂɫs*. They are the creation stories of this particular landscape, of our People. *Captikᵂɫs* guide us, they tell us about the laws, the laws of this land, laws that dictate our lives, our cultural paths, how we behave. Here, in the *tum xúlaʔxᵂ*, these stories guide us. I think it's important that all people understand that coming out of this *tum xúlaʔxᵂ*, this land, there are laws that tell us how to behave on this land. These are cultural laws we have to follow.

The highermost law, the *whuplak'n*, is the law of the land.

It teaches us how we treat everything on this landscape and how to take care of everything on this landscape. The *captikᵂɫs* inform us about what is on the landscape and how it got here. Some of the stories, especially of *Snk̓lip*, Coyote's, debauchery, are around how those things came to be, how we got those particular landscape features. So the top most law is the *whuplak'n*.

Under the *whuplak'n* is the second law which is called *smum iem*.

We are a matrilineal society and a matrilineal People. *Smum iem* means 'belongs to the women.' Everything in this *tum xúlaʔxᵂ* belongs to the women. We own everything, all the land, all the resources, all the children, all the hunger, all the pain, everything. We women play a central role in the laws and how people behave on this landscape. It was and still is our job to help people understand that these laws exist and what their roles are in maintaining a relationship with the landscape.

Understanding these laws and hearing these stories is a process to begin having a relationship with this land. You need to know where you are walking. You need to ask: where is that in the *tum xúlaʔxʷ*? How ancient is that? Our People have been here for thousands and thousands of years. Archaeologists can't understand why there could be a 9,000-year-old tool when it was still an ice age 9,000 years ago. We understand that we had a relationship with the land even when it was covered with ice.

This is where we, Sinixt People, believe we originated.

A traditional person, who was raised in the traditions and cultures of the People, would live inside of these practices and laws. They would go out and gather the Indian foods, do the ceremonies, be engaged in the cultural practices, speak the language. Traditional people still have that connection, even if it's limited to practices like our Winter Dances, which are a key spiritual practice in our yearly cultural cycle.

I'm more of a traditional*ist*, a person who is raised outside cultural connections to traditional ways but learns about their culture from a different, contemporary perspective. To be a traditionalist takes a transformation of a contemporary Indian person through looking for, questing for, ways to live with the land. That person educates themselves in a bigger context, honours peoples' rights to their resources, assists those people and learns their culture and protocols. A traditionalist understands all that has a right to be known, to shine. It's a political perspective about bringing forward all aspects of a culture – governance, ethics, connection to land, everything. It's beyond powwow, it's way beyond activism.

It's about rights and responsibilities as cultural beings.

When you become a traditionalist – or an ally or supporter – you have to understand ceremony, ceremonial protocols, what is right to do when you're visiting someone else's territory, what is respectful. When I've been in other Peoples' traditional territories, I learned to provide whatever service I could, and by providing that service, learned to be humble enough to step back from whatever I see as important. It's their land, it's their issue, it's their culture, their life – so you're there to witness what's going on. If there's some way you can impact in a positive way, can give in a positive way, you're obligated to do that not because you've decided you know what's right. It's not about your brilliant right. You're there to guide them through a process and it's their voice that needs to be heard, their voice, not yours, that needs to define what their culture is, what the issues are.

When you go to be a traditionalist and you have a very contemporary base, you learn those protocols through engaging many different cultural groups and maintaining your behaviour. When you maintain that behaviour, you represent yourself as a People, you represent yourself as a person, youcreate a responsibility to that culture.

That's the path I followed to come home.

The reality is I do what I do – which is tell the stories and share the knowledge – and to have everybody else on the Blood of Life Collective doing what they do, bring the really interesting facets to this project, one of which is this book you're holding right now and its accompanying audio files. I see this as a very engaging and productive way for the settlers in our communities to actually learn some aspect of culture through story. There's more to these stories than, "that wasn't nice of Chickadee, or geez, that Coyote's such a real dumb ass." Maybe you will hear it or you won't hear it, maybe it will tweak your interest or it won't tweak your interest. It's a creative way, if you are going to hear, if you are going to listen, to generate an interest to know a little bit more, to look at those old stories with a little clearer, more sensitive, cultured eye.

**These stories, so many of them,
are from the beginning of time.**

They are so far from where we are in our contemporary perspective. We're stupid if we think we're going to get it and get it right every time. Again, it's about being in the presence of the stories. Conducting and contrasting those realities over a vicious contemporary period of time and also relishing the fact that some of the stories made it. Some of those realities and concepts are there for us to focus on.

So do I believe we have a full spectrum of stories? No. Do I believe that we can generate full concepts of knowing around what these stories actually mean, what is embedded in these stories? No. Our contemporary existences have removed, other than in a most cursory sort of way, that possibility because our culture has been violated, our culture has been colonized. Our culture and perspectives around culture are completely skewed because of the existence that we have to live, completely skewed because of the existence our parents had to live, completely skewed because of the existence our grandparents had to live. That's as far back as I go.

I understand the world my grandmother and grandfather lived in. I understand how hard it was for them to be Indian, to speak Indian. When it was my grandparents' time, they didn't have to go to residential schools but they had to give their children up to residential schools. My mother is a survivor of residential school. The result of that is that we weren't allowed to speak our language. When you speak your language, you have cultural perspective because language is an anchor. Skewed, skewed, skewed. My entire existence is skewed from just that little handful of mentioning. In addition to that there are the layers of racism, the layers of hatred, the layers of self-hatred, the layers of prejudice, the layers of existence while having a target drawn on your forehead, a target drawn on your heart, drawn on your gut, drawn on your back.

The judgments of colonization and those realities become crucial to understanding how limited we are, but within those limitations, how obligated we are to open ourselves up to all of those considerations. When you colonize people, you take away their identity. When you colonize people, you give them a place of being that isn't their place. This takes many forms, but all of them are violent and painful. For those inspired by the move towards reconciliation, the challenge posed in this book is to recognize that the step before reconciliation is truth.

The truth is that we, the Sinixt, exist.
And that here,
there is no reconciliation possible with the Sinixt,
without recognition of the Sinixt.

So this book and the other components of the project – like the podcast audio series, Sinixt Stories: Ancestral Roots, Cultural Seeds – touch a lot of bases. This really creates a swelling of potential for understanding, and a swelling for knowledge. And it can go many places. It's one of those projects where you have one seed and you feed a whole bunch of birds with it. I like that.

THE STORY OF THIS BOOK AND HOW TO EXPLORE IT

The Blood of Life Collective

KL:

It is November 2013 and we are gathered around a campfire at a logging road accessing a mountain currently known as Mount Sentinel, in the range called the Selkirks in the province assigned the name British Columbia. When not warming our butts or throwing broken paletts onto the fire, Marilyn James of the Sinixt and a half-dozen settler folk huddle in lawn chairs, extending our hands towards the fire. The patter of conversations ebb and flow. Occasionally, we eat from the collection of potluck stews and goodies brought by supporters. Now and then, the logging contractor or the police show up to stir the pot of our small blockade.

From time to time, Marilyn James, the *smum iem* Matriarch of the Sinixt People, launches into a story. It can be something as seemingly simple as her remembering her elders, Eva Orr and Alvina Lum, telling the younger folk to pick up any nails left behind from a campfire where lumber scraps have been burned. As she talks, we sift through the ash at the edge of the fire for blackened nails.

Other times, she eyes us with that burning gaze of hers and talks about how to be a good guest in someone else's land. For years, I'd been circling the Sinixt issue, trying to figure out what I could offer to counter the injustice of the erasure of Sinixt rights and

responsibilities in their *tum xúla?x^w*. It is at this fireside that Marilyn and I start talking about this project. I offer up my skills as a writer, activist and cultural worker. Initially, our ideas swirl around attempting to revive *səlxcín*, the profoundly endangered language of the Sinixt. We imagine *səlxcín* words being brought to life through stories connected to those words – huckleberry, salmon, water. We imagine a book.

CATHERINE:

When KL mentions the idea of the project she and Marilyn are cooking up and asks if I will help to record Marilyn James and her daughter, Taress Alexis, telling stories, I feel honoured. I have worked with KL on various projects since 1996, and with Marilyn and Taress starting about the same time. I also have a long history with Kootenay Co-op Radio, a community radio station based in Nelson, BC, where much of the recording will take place. I had thought at first that recording these stories would be the extent of my involvement in the project, but as I sit and listen to the stories and the discussions, I begin to be drawn into the process.

KL:

It is now spring, 2016, and we have secured a grant from the Canada Council's Aboriginal Storyteller Program to begin and we find ourselves perched in front of microphones in a Kootenay

Co-op Radio (KCR) studio. During the two and a half years that have elapsed, the project has shifted and grown in response to funding opportunities and others joining the project. In addition to Marilyn James and myself, Catherine Fisher, long-standing producer of the Sinixt Radio Show at KCR is behind the controls. Amber Santos, artist-educator and collaboration maverick sits next to me and beside Marilyn is Taress Alexis, Marilyn's funny and kind storyteller daughter. Marilyn and Taress are Sinixt, Amber identifies as having a mix of Indigenous and European roots. Catherine and I are the Euro-ish settlers in the group. (Note: a glossary for English terms, like "settler," is at the back of the book.)

The recording begins with Taress telling the story "How Huckleberries Came to Kettle Falls." Next, she tells the iconic "Frog Mountain" story which is familiar to many residents of the Slocan Valley. The next week, it's Marilyn's turn in front of the mic, and we laugh our way through her outrageously animated and funny version of the creation story of the Sinixt, *snx̌ʷntkʷitkʷ*, the Columbia River story. And so on. Week after glorious week.

Those Sinixt stories are the centrepiece of this work. They are available to download or in CD form at www.maapress. ca. (See copyright page for password) We chose not to transcribe the stories from the oral to the written but to let them speak for themselves, honouring their original oral form, as the Sinixt have for millennia in their pithouses and around their campfires. Each chapter of this book is based on one of those stories and each chapter begins with a basic summary of the story being explored. We've chosen to use the original Sinixt names of the Animal Beings who are the main characters of the stories as well as other key terms. *Səlxcín* words are translated the first time they are used in each chapter but after that, you can refer to the glossary at the back.

That spring we managed to have three recording sessions. By the time we started again in September, both the Columbia Kootenay Cultural Alliance and the BC Arts Council with their Arts-based Community Development Project Assistance had stepped up to the plate. Our project, which had gained the name *Blood of Life* from a passing phrase of Marilyn's, was now:

> a multi-disciplinary collaborative arts project designed to present Sinixt culture and teachings to the general public and to foster community relationships between Sinixt and settler (non-Sinixt) peoples through engaging in an artistic process and sharing the resulting body of work with the broader community.

Our recordings were destined to become a 22-part audio series for broadcast/podcast, an illustrated book with accompanying audio files and a public art piece. The overall funding was insufficient to begin work on the public art piece but the audio series and the book were a go.

The grants allowed us to hire youth to mentor in the work of turning Marilyn and Taress's oratory into these other things. Alison Christie joined me, KL, as the writing participant. Axel

McGown was chosen to work with Amber on the art components but ended up wading into the world of audio art also. Kori Doty, Andi Grace and Hannah DeBoer-Smith each worked with the team for short periods of time as well. All of the youth participants identify as settlers. And though each of us was assigned to a certain aspect, in the process of listening to the stories, we became audience, we became curious questioners, we all engaged in learning. We started calling ourselves the Blood of Life Collective.

Each storytelling session was followed by a discussion and these discussions follow the story summaries in this book. What do these sometimes wacky stories mean? After each recording, Marilyn and Taress talked about each story and answered our questions as we grappled to see the world through a radically different lens. These discussions are mostly in Marilyn James' voice unless otherwise noted.

Alison Christie and I tackled the job of turning the spoken word into something that makes sense on the page. We grappled with the intense responsibility, as settlers, of taking an Indigenous person's words and translating them respectfully into writing. We inserted punctuation, moved thoughts around, repeated phrases and words that Marilyn emphasized with her voice. And then, after reading Memory Serves: Oratories by Lee Maracle, we decided to emulate her editor, Smaro Kamboureli, by reading Marilyn's now written oratories back to Marilyn for her approval. Kamboureli writes,

Written oratory, then, opens orality and writing up to one another in ways that simultaneously honour the protocols and values of Indigenous oracy and move Indigenous knowledge forward into the future... it renders it as a living archive of their enduring and continuously unfolding intellectual and spiritual heritage, a compass with which to find the way to the good life.

When reading the discussions about these stories, it is important to remember the ongoing impacts of colonialism and the bureaucratic genocide of the Sinixt. If you perceive anger and bitterness, we hope you will simply listen and take in its passionate insistence. It is the legitimate anger of the oppressed. Its purpose is to wake you up and inspire action. African-American activist Mia McKenzie writes, "In truth, all of what has been gained through anti-oppression movements has been gained with voices as angry as they were calm, as full of rage as they were full of love. Rage has always been part of the fight against the de-humanizing forces of oppression."

A M B E R :

Each story is also accompanied by an image. Through the generosity and openness of Marilyn and Taress, the project team invited artists to consider these stories deeply, and to use their own creative forces to interpret them in the style, medium and design of their choice. All of the artists who responded were settlers or Indigenous to other places. This gesture of collaboration is at the heart of this project. Through this process, there has been an opportunity for dialogue and enagment between local artists and the members of the Blood of Life Collective. Artists listened to stories, created visual ideas, received feedback and then created final works, thus building connection to and relationship with Sinixt culture, as settlers in their *tum xúlaʔxʷ*. Art opens channels to understanding and sensitizing that extend beyond words, building a collective vision of what is, what was and what can be.

KL:

Each chapter ends with A Settler's Reflection. Because of the highly charged nature of the discussions, we decided to include settler voices at the end of each chapter. The purpose of these is not to take up valuable airspace, but to give readers an opportunity to encounter the stories and the discussions in yet another way. After all, the Sinixt worldview is one that is completely different from what cultures steeped in the Judeo-Christian paradigm are used to, especially in the realm of storytelling.

ALISON:

The Western narrative is about a protagonist you can identify with, who is good and right and will prevail in the end, and an antagonist or villain who is bad and wrong and will be destroyed. The result of such a worldview is that good/bad, right/wrong are an easily identifiable binary, which once identified, will result in justice. The problem with this is, of course, that no such simplistic binary actually exists, with the full range of possible circumstances and outcomes of life being far more vast and complex. Told from a Sinixt perspective, these stories demonstrate over and over the vast and complex nature of life, morality, teachings and lessons in a way that may cause cognitive dissonance when reading through a colonial lens of narrative and storytelling.

KL:

Initially, Alison and I set out to write the Settler Reflections on our own but then realized multiple voices would enable the greatest diversity of encounters with the material. The Reflections are written by people who were eager to engage in this project in the spirit of "start where you are." That meant encountering whatever reactions or ideas, feelings or thoughts, or resistances to acknowledging Sinixt realities people had. The ideas that inform the current colonial situation were generated for a purpose and by looking more closely and seeking to open up respectful conversations, perhaps we can discover the ways in which these old ideas no longer serve us, as individuals, as communities and as a country.

CATHERINE:

The other major component of this project is "Sinixt Stories: Ancestral Roots, Cultural Seeds," the audio series. Hearing Marilyn and Taress tell these stories and discuss them afterwards was an amazing listening experience in itself. Taking these recordings and adding texture and shape to them added layers to the listening experience, because when you create a sound documentary, you learn to listen in a whole new way. The audio series began being broadcast on KCR in Nelson, BC in October of 2017. To listen to the podcasts, go to www.kootenaycoopradio.com and follow the links. The 21 episodes of the Audio Series are different from the book and the accompanying audio files/

CD, though based on the same stories and discussion sessions. They merit a listen whether you read this book or not.

KL:

One of the questions we encountered along the way was – why were we, settlers, doing this work and not exclusively the Sinixt? Due to their bureaucratic extinction in part, Sinixt voices are few in the Canadian portion of *tum xúlaʔxʷ*. Also, as settlers, we need to take responsibility for grappling with the effects of colonization and loss of Indigenous Culture. Through educating ourselves on the impacts of colonization, we can find ways of engaging with Indigenous People and culture that are about being in service rather than continuing to take. So when Marilyn and Taress invited us to join them, we said yes. Every step was guided and overseen by them. We grappled regularly with what it meant to be settlers doing this work and how to do it honourably. Marilyn and Taress retain complete control over the content and even the form of the work.

None of the non-Sinixt members of the Blood of Life Collective will ever be "experts" on the Sinixt. Indigenous Peoples do not need outsider experts. Nor have we been empowered to take this material and use it for our own personal purposes. Cultural appropriation continues the theft and devastation of colonialism. Indigenous cultures and spiritualities were not put here for our use; they belong to the Peoples who birthed them, for them to share as they choose.

AMBER:

Taking part in this project is part of a life-long journey to decolonize my own life and worldview and to honour the Indigenous Peoples of the place I call home. As a child and a youth of Indigenous and European ancestry growing up here, any mention of being "Indian" inspired negative stereotypes and derogatory comments. I continue to peel back the layers of the onion that is my ancestry through family stories that emerge through the building of relationship, healing and the elusive quality of time and its impact on our experiences. The German, Italian, French, Saulteaux, Cree and Métis roots that created me and the ancestors whom I honour, stretch far from the place I call home, where my childhood memories are and where I feel a sense of belonging and community. I grapple with my sense of belonging here.

I left this community to study and travel in other places, mostly the northeast of Brazil where I met my soulmate. There I learned about northeast Brazilian cultures of resistance and participated in social art movements, stirring me deeply to be part of the movement towards respecting all cultures' right to exist and thrive and to resist all forms of oppression, wherever I reside. When I moved back to the community in 2009, my ear perked up at any mention of the Sinixt people. I slowly pieced together what I could about Sinixt culture, people, ways of life, beliefs and teachings.

Being part of this project means being an ally to support the resurgence of the Sinixt people. I remember hearing about how "this valley was too sacred and mystical for Indians to reside here," an urban myth and colonial lie that was repeated through diverse resources and until today, I hear repeated from others.

I connect to this landscape, and want to know the people of this landscape. I want to see the Sinixt people thrive, to support by being an ally with the tools that I work with, art and education. Learning from the Sinixt is an opportunity to see this landscape in a different way and to serve this landscape by taking on a role of protecting and stewarding it, by learning from the people who have done this for millennia.

KL:

In the process of working on the book, the dire need for educational materials about the Sinixt in schools from the elementary level to college and university became evident. Teachers we met with conveyed urgency about getting this material out into the world. In response to the recommendations of Canada's Truth and Reconciliation Commission, schools were being asked to include Indigenous materials at all levels, in all subjects. Because of the extinct status of the Sinixt and their exile south of the border, few materials were available. Many teachers offered their help in practical ways and the Supplementary Resource Kit that is now available in digital form is a result of this. Please visit the Blood of Life Facebook page or www.maapress.ca for a link to this resource.

The settler Blood of Life Collective members feel profoundly honoured and blessed to have participated in this work. To Marilyn and Taress, we offer our deep gratitude. May this work help the Sinixt People and your Culture resurge from the ongoing devastation of colonialism and bureaucratic extinction. *Lim limpt, lim limpt, lim limpt.*

SNX̌ᵂNTKᵂITKᵂ, COLUMBIA RIVER

Snk̓lip, Coyote, met *Sq́it*, Rain, a beautiful, humble woman and tried to win her over. She rejected him but *Snk̓lip* persisted in trying to get *Sq́it* to share her gifts and fall in love with him. Finally, he enchanted her with a song until the rain began to fall. It fell and fell until the water began to rise and *Sq́it* picked *Snk̓lip* up and carried him all the way to Ocean, her beautiful cousin. Snk̓lip immediately fell for Ocean. Broken-hearted, *Sq́it* threw her heart to where they came from and created a pathway of love, *Snx̌ʷntkʷitkʷ*, the Columbia River. *Sq́it* demanded promised gifts from *Snk̓lip* and he pulled out his hair and threw it next to *Sq́it*'s river and they turned into salmon runs, animals and landscape features. From his heart, he took out the Sinixt People to put next to *Sq́it*'s heart to revere, respect and love *Sq́it*. He promised to return one day to make everything right. To this day, the Sinixt People await his return.

Story told by Taress Alexis

Art by Tyler Toews

MARILYN:

This Sinixt creation story would have been told over the winter months in pit houses during the storytelling season where they would have talked about all of the things that used *Snx̌ʷntkʷitkʷ*, the Columbia River system.

**The story would have lasted for days,
or even weeks.**

It would have described how various beings use *Snx̌ʷntkʷitkʷ*, how they use it, who comes to the water and when they come to the water. The storyteller would have talked about how to make way for your bear neighbours to come fishing, how to create access for the kingfishers and how to watch these beings use the water and how we, the Sinixt, maintain our relationship with the same body of water. It's being informed of that usage through story. How you have a relationship with water and respect that water.

And, of course, each storyteller would have had a way to wake up their audience. After hearing so much about what's available, what's using the water, etc., occasionally people would start nodding off and so the storyteller takes creative licence to wake the audience up. Every storyteller has creative licence to put their personal spin on stories and that's what I did here.

Wake up! Wake up!
***Snk̓lip*, Coyote, is here!**
Crazy coyote, (hee hee)
***lewd*,**
crude,
goofy, skirt-chaser,
will wake you up!

One of the stories about how we came to be is the *Snx̌ʷntkʷitkʷ* Story. *Snx̌ʷntkʷitkʷ* is a major landscape feature within this *tum xúlaʔxʷ*, our territory, and not only within this *tum xúlaʔxʷ* but it is the uppermost region of the river and thus would dictate all of the salmon culture practice downstream, which takes in the entire river system.

When they talk about Salmon Chiefs, they really are talking about the Sinixt People.

We're the People who would have dictated when anyone downstream got to fish when the runs established themselves in the river. And it would have been the Sinixt People who would have given the word for the fishing to begin. This dictated the survival of all the Indians in terms of salmon as a major food source. That's a pretty powerful position to hold.

Control over this water, these rivers, represents a high level of affluence and power.

Looking back at history, we see David Thompson frantically trying to find the Columbia and to claim it before any of those others, like Lewis and Clark, could claim it for the other side. The actual issue against the Sinixt People, being the only People on *Snx̌ʷntkʷitkʷ* in Canada, begins at that time. Then, we experienced more waves of settlers, we experienced the great waves of dying, we experienced the settling of our region by the settler culture. We then have the establishment of the 49th parallel, the establishment of the USA, the establishment of Canada. As the relationship progresses, *Snx̌ʷntkʷitkʷ*'s southern stem comes to belong to USA, the northern stem comes to belong to Canada. Alongside this, the numbers of the Sinixt People who occupied their Northern territory diminish dramatically. As the settlers grew more entrenched and the numbers of Sinixt People occupying the region became less and less through military force as well as being eradicated and relegated to the southern aspect of their territory, it became easier to have control over *Snx̌ʷntkʷitkʷ*.

Pre-European contact, the Sinixt People would have been a powerful influence.

Because of that influence, the government declared the Sinixt extinct in 1956 prior to the signing of the Columbia River Treaty. Now, of course, the Canadian government holds all of the control of *Snx̌ʷntkʷitkʷ* in Canada. It's no coincidence that just prior to the signing of the Columbia River Treaty between the USA and Canada, the Canadian government declared the Sinixt People extinct in Canada. It completely eradicated the Sinixt ability to come back to our territory, carry out our responsibilities, exercise influence and maintain our seasonal-rounds in the northern part of our territory.

The fact that the Columbia River Treaty was designed to take control over the waters, to make money, to create the dams, to stop the salmon migrating up *Snx̌ʷntkʷitkʷ*, is key. If they could eradicate the Indians, they could do away with the importance of mitigating the rights of the Sinixt People. Having Indian People here creates a whole plethora of problems. It means you have to consult, it means the Indians would not have allowed the fish to be eradicated. They would have had to make fish ladders on those dams on *Snx̌ʷntkʷitkʷ* because we are a Salmon People. The other reality is that when you control that river, you control power, you control the economics.

And Indian People were just in the way.
We were in the way.

We had an established reservation at Oatscott, just above Edgewood, straight up the river from Castlegar. The Indian Act was targeting Indian People for disenfranchisement. The Sinixt People who were in the region who had married white men were no longer considered Indian. You can go on and on about the horrors of the Indian Act: residential school, disenfranchisement, 60s baby scoop. If we fast-forward to 1991, when Minister of Indian Affairs Ron Irwin was asked why the Sinixt were declared extinct, he wrote in a letter to a supporter: "For the purposes of the Indian Act, the Sinixt were declared extinct but they never ceased to exist as a tribal group." So we were actually targeted

and focussed upon to further the government's means to gain control and have the power over *Snx̌ʷntkʷitkʷ* without any undue and unnecessary involvement of Indian People.

Under the laws of colonization, they have to consult, they have to make treaties – commit all the atrocities they do – but they have to do it under a treaty process. They weren't even civilized enough or compassionate enough to create those aspects of consultation and compassion for the Indian People, the Sinixt, who were from this region. The government said:

Let's just declare them extinct since
we have laws that allow us to do that.

Up to 99% of the archaeological sites along *Snx̌ʷntkʷitkʷ* in Canada were flooded and eradicated as a result of the building of the Keenleyside Dam at Castlegar. So not only did they eradicate us physically from the landscape, they attempted to eradicate our historical record of being here. It's a law, you can't go to a sacred Indian burial site and dig it up. But when you lower water levels in a reservoir (drawdown) like the one behind Keenleyside Dam, people will go in there and pick up arrowheads. The water scrubs down the land and exposes new artifacts each year and they can be documented and GPS'ed but they're not considered viable or valid artifacts. They cannot be attributed to the very land they come from because of the nature of how they're exposed. And it's completely legal for people to just pick them up. Massive collections have been attributed to people who have collected artifacts at old burial sites, old village sites.

Our *captik^{w}łs*, our creation stories, tell us that we were created on the headwaters of *Snx̌^{w}ntk^{w}itk^w* so our oldest, most ancient records would have been there.

They've eradicated our most ancient records.

Even at the Lemon Creek archaeological dig, with the 12,500-year-old carbon dating that places us on the land, those would have been secondary placements to our existence along *Snx̌^{w}ntk^{w}itk^w* where we came to be as a People. Hamilton College has been conducting field studies at the Lemon Creek site for over a decade now. (See Lemon Creek story.)

As Indian People, we have a place to be, that's where we can create our prosperity, that's where we create our existence and survival. When they created the dams, they diminished the Sinixt place of existence. When they began flooding up behind Grand Coulee Dam, they actually flooded the very village of Inchelium where many Sinixt, who had already been displaced many times, were living. They had to pick up this old dude who was sitting on his porch, because he was just going to sit there and drown. He didn't want to leave his place.

With the dam came the eradication of the salmon, came the eradication of place and being. And of course, the big loss of those salmon really hit the Sinixt hard. They held a Ceremony of Tears to note the passing of their time as a People with that species, their responsibility to take care of that being. The realization of what that meant would have happened in the mid to late fifties.

It was heartbreaking because so many people relied on the salmon.

The Ceremony of Tears is like anything else you don't talk about. If you've ever been around a veteran who has experienced post-traumatic stress, they don't sit around and talk about the traumas of war. They don't talk about it at all. That was part of the legacy of the post-traumatic stress on Indian People. We didn't talk about the loss of the salmon and the Ceremony of Tears. We didn't talk about our Moms or Dads or Aunties or Uncles being taken away to residential schools and being raped, or about those who got beaten to death. Even the occasional stories about the runaways are whispered stories of a very terrifying, tragic existence.

I see the building of the dams as the biggest blow to salmon stocks, to wild salmon runs up *Snx̌^{w}ntk^{w}itk^w*, because certainly those species at the very headwaters of *Snx̌^{w}ntk^{w}itk^w* would have represented the strongest, oldest, most ancient beings anywhere on this river system. Salmon represented the largest renewable resource anywhere on the planet. Dam the river and you cut off all of those things that inform the entire system.

Cut off the head of something
– which is what they did
when they damed *Snx̌^{w}ntk^{w}itk^w* -
No brain,
No resilience.
No sustainability.
River destroyed.
Destroyed forever.

And it's sad to now hear so many people cheering for and wanting to promote the return of the salmon up *Snx̌ʷntkʷitkʷ*. I'm not a fan of doing that because *Snx̌ʷntkʷitkʷ* is toxic now. The Pacific Ocean is toxic now. Our responsibility is to our resident fish – we have many salmonid species that need taking care of, like the *kíkniʔ*, kokanee, that are failing now. We need to enhance those runs and make sure those landlocked salmonids have the opportunity to sustain themselves within this *tum xúlaʔxʷ* and represent non-polluted and pristine food sources for people. Many people of this region rely upon fisheries to some degree to sustain themselves nutritionally. The fisheries have failed in many rivers in the system like *Sɫuqin*, the Slocan River. There are many things have caused that, like the Lemon Creek fuel spill.

To me, this stem of the Columbia River represents much more of what's happened to us socially, politically, environmentally. It represents what's happening to this entire region. When you begin counting the dams on *Snx̌ʷntkʷitkʷ* and its tributaries – there's upward of 456 dams, which allows Lewiston, Idaho to be a seaport. When you reconfigure a body of water, a river system to sustain that kind of usage, you have really skewed this system beyond repair in so many ways.

Beyond repair.
Beyond repair.

This place that we now call the Inland Temperate Rainforest is changing in other ways too. The levels of rain that we used to experience in Vallican in the Slocan Valley have changed dramatically from the amounts we'd get before. We're losing and changing those levels of precipitation that cause it to be a unique environment. So the *Snx̌ʷntkʷitkʷ* I remember from stories from when I was a kid, is no more. I remember my father talking about when they were 'young fellas,' that they were able to step across the very beginning of *Snx̌ʷntkʷitkʷ* at Canal Flats. Of course they dredged all of that up and created a completely different scenario than those swamps and wetlands that used to be there. *Sq́it* is a great being and I see this landscape changing in incredible and profound ways in terms of what she created and what she represents on this landscape.

When working with this story and transcribing Marilyn James' eloquent discussion, I struggled with punctuation: behind statements like "destroyed" or "beyond repair" do I put a period or a question mark? I wanted the question mark but feared Marilyn would want a period. My job was not to put anything in her mouth, not even a squiggle above a dot so I put both options in my first draft and took it back to Marilyn for a decision. What the squiggle above the dot, ?, versus the period brings up for me are the notions of hope and trust.

That *Snx̌ʷntkʷitkʷ*, the Columbia River system, is profoundly damaged is evident. And it's not just the river that has been impoverished by the building of the dams, but the entire upper *Snx̌ʷntkʷitkʷ* ecosystem. Those salmon runs nourished the land, the trees and all its creatures for millennia. We can know the ages of old bear bones and even trees from this area by seeing whether they have the isotopes of salmon food in them or not.

We know that the Sinixt People grieved the end of the salmon runs personally and collectively. The faces of the women in the pictures taken at the Ceremony of Tears speak volumes. A great migration of life that had gone on for thousands and thousands of years, over – Bang! – just like that. It's difficult to imagine the changes wreaked on this landscape, as well as the grief of the people who loved and relied on the salmon since the beginning of time.

What kind of repair could take place, or perhaps more aptly – what kind of evolution could happen – if we changed the way we collectively interact with this place? What if we returned to the laws of this land – the *whuplak'n*, the *smum iem* – and forged a new relationship as settlers with all the beings who have inhabited *Snx̌ʷntkʷitkʷ* for millennia? I do not put much stock in hope but I do trust that the Earth continues to evolve and change. I also deeply trust in the wisdom of Indigenous People about the lands they have emerged from. Does trust + trust = healing? Perhaps, but this trust cannot be passive; it must be active, listening, responsible. It is about our ability to respond to the Sinixt, our ability to respond to climate change, our ability to respond to the landscape where we have made our homes, our ability to adapt and grow and cultivate resilience personally and in our communities. Are we able?

KL KIVI

SẂAŔAḰXN, FROG MOUNTAIN

A long, long, long time ago, there was a drought – everything on the landscape started to go away. The village elder feared his People would perish, and talked to them about leaving, although he was too old himself. Some would stay behind with him, and some would go, so their culture could be preserved for the next generations. The elder went to pray and fast. A little frog, *Sẃaŕakxn*, appeared and told him, "if you dig caves for your People, you will all survive". So that's what the People did, unsure if they would survive, especially when the snow came. *Sẃaŕakxn* began to appear, offering themselves to the People. The snow melted, the drought was over and the People could return to the land. One of the tiny *Sẃaŕakxn* hopped and grew into *Sẃaŕakxn*, the mountain, becoming a symbol of the love the frogs showed for Sinixt People.

Story told by Taress Alexis, learned from Eva Orr.

Art by Moe Lyons

This story informs me of how long our culture has been on this landscape: since the mountains were forming. This story goes on long before us, long before my lifetime, *q̓sápiʔ, q̓sápiʔ, q̓sápiʔ,* long before my ability to speak that language or even know much about it.

A lot of how our animals are named, is how you would think of them, or how they sound. So if you think of *Sẃaŕakxn,* the frogs, saying *Sẃaŕakxn,* it's another language of the landscape. The mountain is frog. You don't say Frog Mountain, you say Frog.

Sẃaŕakxn.
Since the mountains were forming.

I know word association in terms of the landscape, like *x̌aʔx̌aʔ,* that makes it sacred.

An aspect we need to focus on in terms of storytelling, is introducing those words to the landscape, and creating resources for those words – getting people interested in the language because ours is a dying dialect. Salish is a thriving language but there's many dialects. The Okanagan, *nsəlxcín,* has lots of speakers, but the Sinixt dialect, *səlxcín,* does not.

And it's part of our responsibility as Sinixt People to get the language back on the landscape through trying to create those opportunities for people to learn more, know more. The more people know and learn the better. Currently, the dialect isn't dead, it's stuttered.

səlxcín.
Since the mountains were forming.

Maybe there's a speaker or two, but a lot of the speakers that say they're speaking the Sinixt language are really speaking *nsəlxcín,* Okanagan. A lot of the words I speak probably aren't pronounced properly, and that's part of my story. My story is that my people who were fluent speakers wouldn't allow me to hear it or speak it. So when I was little, whenever they were speaking – and I loved hearing them speak – I'd have to sneak around them or they'd holler at me and chase me away.

səlxcín

And I'm the child of a survivor of residential schools. My mom was telling stories with the other gals about what it was like, what the punishments were like for speaking your language in the residential school.

səlxcín

So they never wanted us to know the language, to even have it as a possibility for us to be punished like they were for speaking the language. Everybody speaks English now. The opportunities I did have, I was very stealthy and sneaky. I would hide under the trailer when they were out tanning hides behind the shack so I could listen to them. But just listening to them wasn't like speaking to them.

səlxcín

I encourage people to tell the story because it brings more awareness to the landscape. When we first moved here, nobody knew about frog mountain. But then through story telling people started to see *Sẃaŕaḱxn* for what it really was, and that makes me happy.

Since the mountains were forming.

I don't tell any stories other than Sinixt stories and I have always felt a responsibility to tell certain stories as a Sinixt person. When I first heard this story I thought of how relevant it is in this day and age, for how we should be taking care of things, how we should consciously know what's here on the landscape and make sure there's a place for it. Because so much is being pushed off the landscape. Knowing we were a Salmon Culture and knowing the dams have taken the fish away, and that's no longer a part of this landscape.

As the People of this land
who have been declared extinct,
we know exactly what's been pushed
from this landscape.

Story is a way to inform us of what really had a right and a responsibility to be on this landscape that we impacted.

So I have a responsibility to tell story.
Responsibility to land, responsibility to water.
Responsibility to *Sẃaŕaḱxn*
to *səlxcín*

I hope that whoever tells this story, tells it with respect and the dignity it deserves. At least be able to refer to it as a Sinixt story; there's an actual mountain – tell the story to compel people to want to see the mountain,

Sẃaŕaḱxn.

These stories aren't copyrighted, they're passed down like culture and tradition, you can't own that. However, you need permission to talk about people's ancestors and what happened to them.

As the People of this land
who have been declared extinct,
we know exactly what's been pushed
from this landscape.

People need to acknowledge where the story comes from, and give back with some level of integrity.

This story informs me of how long
our culture has been on this landscape.
Since the mountains were forming.

31

A SETTLER'S REFLECTION:

Sẃaŕaḱxn.

"A lot of how our animals are named, is how they sound." *Sẃaŕaḱxn.* I hear frog in these delicate rolling syllables. It strikes me the depth of relationship to landscape and creatures that must exist in order for names to form in a way that resonates with their essence. *Sẃaŕaḱxn.* I say it out loud and feel the pulse of something tiny and a bit jumpy in this word, as if it leaps from the human tongue the way frogs leap their way through swampy forest paths.

I am lost in the immeasurably delicate beauty of one word that can imbue relationship in such deep and intricate ways. Then, like the brick from walls of a residential school being smashed through that relationship, the part of the story comes where the language of this landscape being spoken is met with punishment, torture, forceful silencing; the mouths of the people broken, a deadening silence lingering where a moment ago the profundity of intimate connection was felt.

When I think about this story and the relationship of land and people, I can grasp only a surface understanding of what is being offered by *Sẃaŕaḱxn* to ensure the survival of the Sinixt. My colonial public school education that values proper English grammar and correct spelling taught me only the importance of getting it right. The idea of connection to place through the meaning of language is just that: an idea. And with that lack of connection comes a profound severance from land as the sustainer of all life. I've been taught that

mountains, trees, rivers and critters are all separate, categorizable "things" that only have meaning by way of their usefulness to human beings. The English language supports this disconnect, as language and culture mutually cooperate and inform one another. In order to destroy relationship to culture, relationship to language must be forbidden.

I've been taught there is power in words. Can speaking the language of a landscape breathe life into the attempted erasure of Sinixt culture and People? What is our responsibility as settlers to support this process? For me, it is a revival of something ancient, something that was born on this territory and continues to exist in rock and wind and stream. The responsibility of anyone whose life is sustained by these forces, which means all of us, is to learn to call someone by their true name. To remember who they are.

So if you think of *Sẃaŕaḱxn*,
the frogs saying *Sẃaŕaḱxn*,
it's another language of the landscape.
The mountain is frog.
You don't say frog mountain,
you say frog.
Sẃaŕaḱxn

ALISON CHRISTIE

32

HOW THE STURGEON-NOSED CANOE CAME TO BE

x̌ʷʕʷaylxʷ, Fox married a beautiful woman who made him very happy. Every morning x̌ʷʕʷaylxʷ's wife would go down to the little creek, *cwix*, and speak to the water. She began to notice x̌ʷʕʷaylxʷ sneaking around following her, waiting for her to show she was being disloyal. One day Sturgeon, *ćmtus,* leaped from the water and took Mrs. Fox far away downstream to his own lodge, at *k'tunk*, Kettle Falls. *ćmtus* sent Mrs. Duck and Mrs. Goose, *kw'sixw,* to steal Mrs. Fox's belongings from her own lodge so she could be happy with him. Sturgeon pulled a scale off his nose that curls up into a point, and told them to dive in with his scale. While gathering Mrs. Fox's belongings, x̌ʷʕʷaylxʷ overheard their conversation and followed them back downstream. x̌ʷʕʷaylxʷ and his wife hopped on Sturgeon's nose scale and returned home happily together.

Story told by Marilyn James

Art by Amber Santos

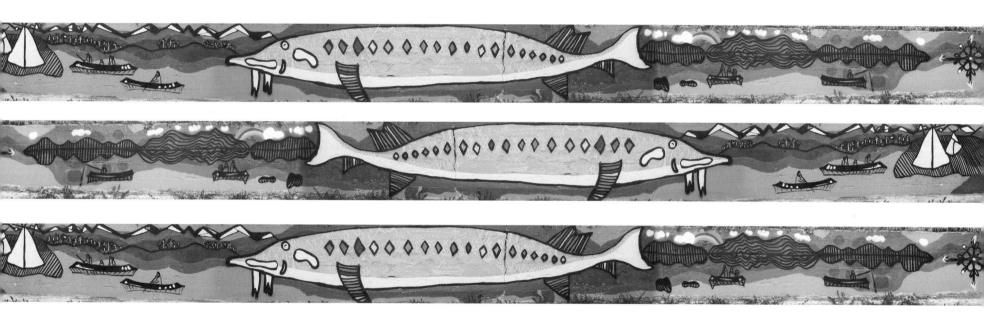

RELATIONSHIP BETWEEN STURGEON AND THE CANOE

If you've ever witnessed fish scales, when you take off the larger fish scale, they have a tendency to create a kind of curl to them. The sturgeon nose of the sturgeon-nosed canoe is the physical form of this with its pointed nose. When Sturgeon takes the curl off his nose for Mrs. Goose and Mrs. Duck, it creates a certain movement in the water – that's our design. That's a specific Sinixt design utilized in this area because of the large bodies of water we had to traverse within our *tum xúla?xʷ*, our territory.

Within huge bodies of water like Kootenay Lake, Upper and Lower Arrow Lakes, Slocan Lake, or Trout Lake even, the "Lake Effect" is created. They talk about this back east too. There's a lot of roughness to these waters. That Sinixt design could handle those rough waters. The other reality is, Sinixt People are named after a fish, the Bull Trout, *ʕayckst*, and have a great relationship with all aquatic life. Sturgeon is a very ancient being the Sinixt related to and saw as an aquatically adept creature that survived over a long, long period of time. Where other things came and went, Sturgeon had longevity, and a special relationship with the Sinixt People in this regard.

BEAUTY

This is a picture of *smum iem*: how you help in a village situation. There were so many people that were capable of doing the work and being of service in a village. Berry picking, gathering bark for basket making or tule mats, medicine gathering, root digging, wood gathering; there was always something to be done. Knowing that by being of service, that service comes back to serve you and your need, in whatever realm. When we talk about being beautiful inside and out, how you behave and present yourself to your people is part of that.

**Beauty lies in how you are
of service to your community.**

JEALOUSY

Jealousy can completely transform a person and their character. If you're not vigilant about this condition it will consume you. It will consume your behaviour, your life; it will change things in your life profoundly if that beast gets a hold of you.

TREACHERY

Of course, there is the wickedness and treachery of someone always trying to benefit from another's downfall, oppression, or fear. When Mrs. Fox is taken by Sturgeon, Mrs. Goose and Mrs. Duck are eager to help Sturgeon in his quest to keep her, even though they were supposed to be friends of Mrs. Fox.

There's always someone trying to benefit out of another's downfall. That's a pretty common human characteristic and there are people who consider themselves friends based on that treachery, and I think that's always existed. Mrs. Duck and Mrs.

Goose are able to convince themselves they are actually helping Mrs. Fox to be happier, even though she is stuck at Sturgeon's against her own will.

I think it's a condition that exists today, and that we don't teach our children how to deal with these levels of treachery and treacherous behaviour. We don't teach them how you get around it, accept it, recognize it, or deal with it. Responding to treacherous behaviour becomes part of community acknowledgment. In this day and age, isolated approaches to behaviour don't give us the backup we need to respond to the emotional realities we deal with every day, that our children need to learn to deal with.

Duck and Goose are a symptom of community; in every community, they are present. What we have now is tolerance around certain behaviour that makes it okay to suck the energy out of the bigger things that need to get done. In the traditional context, we would have recognized people who were sucking energy from the group for what they are, but today people can be suckers, and we rationalize it as okay; they have a good heart. If people aren't contributing, but we allow them to benefit, it is a drain on community resources. Coyote is just blatant about who he is, and he's crude. "Who cares about your wife? There's more to life – forget about her!" All the time, he's being upfront and complaining. You know what you're dealing with. That guy is a scoundrel, a scam, and you'll never get a lick of work out of him; you know that. But Mrs. Goose and Mrs. Duck really define treachery because they're supposed to be Mrs. Fox's friends, and they convince even themselves what good friends they are, through betraying her for their own benefit.

FICKLENESS

There are a lot of stories of how women find themselves in emotional commitment. That's a fickle state, it can go this way or that way and it doesn't matter who your partner is and how much they provide for you, you can always find someone else to be enamored with. Sometimes, being attracted to another can produce its own challenges in terms of your relationship.

We can look at those challenges. You might lust after someone, someone might spark your eye, but give it some thought. Are you going to end up in a better place; are you going to be happy there? No matter where you go, or how happy you think you might be, there's always something to find not quite right with where you're at and use that as an excuse for needing it to be different.

RELATIONSHIP AND LANDSCAPE

These stories resonate with how people need to create perspectives of landscape. Where we're at in the world, what mountains mean to us, and how we should be guided in our lives are all influenced by landscape. The relevance creates a lens for people to look through and begin processing landscape relationships. Because these stories are so filled with character references, you need to have a relationship with those characters and understand them to create perspectives of truth. Everyone creates the images and emotion of the story in a very personal way. When you create perspectives of truth, you begin the process of creating relationship. You don't get to relationship without truth. You can't.

Everything that isn't based upon a truth
is a fallacy and you can't go forward.
It's skewed.
It's not a relationship then;
it's an invention.

A SETTLER'S REFLECTION:

Initially, the discussion of this story made me feel discouraged. Although very symbolic and clever elements are present here, there are also the nasty bits of human character – betrayal and acting solely to benefit yourself. There is the issue of Mrs. Fox being treated like property, married first to Fox and then stolen by Sturgeon. My inner feminist alarm bell was going through the roof with outrage at the female character being kidnapped and rescued by husbands/other male fish. However...

I keep coming back to a place of reminding myself these stories survived from their original form, squeezed through the colonially imposed lens of patriarchal gender roles, and still maintain immense value and teachings of traditional culture. I'm curious about a culture in which there were traditional gender roles, but not ones that painted females as inferior to males. My only point of reference in this lifetime is Western patriarchy, and that makes such a culture difficult for me to imagine.

This story seems to speak to the nature of relationships. There are so many ways of being in relationship to one another; of what a larger community in balance looks like. Despite my initial reactions to the gendered character portrayals, when I sink down deeper into the themes that have maybe always existed in human communities – beauty, treachery, jealousy, envy, relationship to landscape. And from this place there is deep value in being able to look at each of these qualities in turn, to consider how they speak to the health of the people and integrity of how a community functions.

The characters in these stories portray aspects of humanity that continue to play themselves out. In this way a thread of connection to something so old, that has trickled down the ancestral lines to find continued relevance in modern existence, remains unbroken. Although the container of a culture that responds to the ongoing maintenance of community has been eroded, the characters portrayed in these stories provide a way of relating to the interconnection of all human beings.

ALISON CHRISTIE

WHALE, FOX AND COYOTE

x̌ʷʕʷaylxʷ, Fox, married a beautiful woman from the village and provided well for his wife. But while fussing over herself looking at her reflection in the water, a water-being thought she was fussing for him. *x̌ʷʕʷaylxʷ*'s brother *Snk̓lip*, Coyote, noticed her behaviour and alerted *x̌ʷʕʷaylxʷ*. *x̌ʷʕʷaylxʷ* witnessed the water-being take his wife away to a place on *Snx̌ʷntkʷitkʷ*, the Columbia River. Mrs. Duck and Mrs. Goose, who had talked to Mrs. Fox in her new home, came to gather things for her that she needed in her new life. *Snk̓lip* and *x̌ʷʕʷaylxʷ* killed Mrs. Duck and Mrs. Goose in order to disguise themselves and set out to find Mrs. Fox. When they found the water-being, who is Whale, *x̌ʷʕʷaylxʷ* killed him and sent him downstream. That is how the whales were relegated to the salt water. And Mrs. Fox resumed her life with her husband and her people.

Story told by Marilyn James, from *Coyote Stories*.

Art by Amber Santos

Before scientists actually discovered whale remains at Dry Falls in Washington State, they pooh-poohed away the idea of an Indian oral history, that two females and a male whale swam up the Columbia River in ancient times. They said,

**That could never happen,
there's no way that could have ever happened,
there's no evidence whatsoever that it took place.**

Yet, there's a *captik^wł*, an ancient story, about how it happened, that monsters – that's how they were referred to – came up the Columbia River. Lo and behold! Fox and Coyote and Whale! It's basically the same story as the Sturgeon-nosed canoe story, almost exactly the same, except for this significant difference.

Of the three whales found at Dry Falls, there was one male, an adult female and one young female. It was a little family pod that actually came up the Columbia River. This was a very long distance from the ocean. Those discoveries didn't happen until recently whereas these stories have existed for millennia within our culture. Understanding these stories and now receiving shards of biological and archaeological evidence that back up the stories confirms our *captik^wł*.

My misinterpretation was that the Great Falls they were referring to was the same as the one in the Sturgeon-nosed Canoe story, where Sturgeon takes Fox's wife to *k'tunk*, Kettle Falls. I had assumed the Great Falls referred to in this story was also Kettle Falls. But no, it was Dry Falls, which is no longer part of the Columbia River system.

**Dry Falls is part of
the ancient pathway of *Snx̌^wntk^witk^w*
that eventually changed.**

Snx̌^wntk^witk^w doesn't go that way anymore; it turns at the Colville Rez (Colville Confederated Tribes Reservation), in Washington, and swings way past Wenatchee. But it used to go straight down over the Columbia Basin instead of the bends it takes now. Dry Falls is where the main body of water flowed when the initial glacial melt happened, when the big ice dam broke, forcing the water down. It was the initial path of the *Snx̌^wntk^witk^w*.

It's interesting, the geologist Lesley Anderton said, "Glaciers are secondary to rivers." When the Earth heated up then cooled down it began to create fissures. Those fissures became the rivers and those rivers shaped the land more than the glaciers did. The water that flowed always flowed, it flowed under glaciers, it flowed through glaciers, it became glaciers. Then when the land allowed it, it created its pathways even deeper set than before. To me, an important aspect of understanding landscape history is through geology and how land is formed. Which makes *Snx̌^wntk^witk^w* more ancient, more set, more determined, than all the glaciers that existed – all the three or four glacial eras that ever happened here.

Snx̌^wntk^witk^w is different now. There's no water at Dry Falls anymore, just a huge cliff that the water used to run over. These are puzzles we still think about. Over a big span of time, the big falls could very well have been Dry Falls and not Kettle Falls. Many ancient beings have been found there.

**Blue Rhinoceros,
shape in the stone, turned upside down.
And Whale. And Whale!**

Yet everyone – settlers and academics – pooh-poohed away the idea, the idea of Indian oral history. Pooh-poohed the ancient stories. To me, it speaks to the occupation of a land at a time when the people who lived here knew the river to be at a different location than it actually is now. The stories reflect that long period of time when the river had its different formations and paths. Those stories relate back to that time.

It doesn't seem realistic that whales would swim up the *Snx̌ʷntkʷitkʷ*, but if you imagine that great ice dam breaking and the amount of water it must have taken to form those falls and the great basalt valleys that were carved out by that water, it's possible. There must have been a tremendous amount of water flowing down at one time that could have easily accommodated whales swimming up.

It happened.

I was excited to see the Sturgeon-nosed Canoe story in another form – now it's about Whale. Little did I know that it was going to be related in another way to our history, to our time with the river. It relates to a time when beings, creatures, were trying to find their place on the landscape. Was the whale going to be a fresh-water creature or a salt water creature? Where did they end up? Those stories relate to the eventual placement of animals on the land.

**Those stories are ancient beings,
those stories speak to human evolution.
Those stories are ancient beings,
knowing about things,
like time and space.
Those stories relate back to this land.
Ancient. Related.**

In a bigger context, the story was about how creatures were finding their place to be on the planet. Like with the buffalo story (see Coyote and the Buffalo story), it's about how those choices dominate your relationship to the landscape. What if whales had been allowed to be fresh-water beings? Maybe we'd be responsible for the demise of the whales in the Columbia River system with all the dams.

Maybe in the grand scheme of things we were meant to be responsible not for the Whale People but for the Salmon People. Maybe that's who we could be responsible for in this *tum xúlaʔxʷ*, our territory, and who this *tum xúlaʔxʷ* could support.

**The stories are a key to
the shaping of the landscape.**

It was always a puzzle as there were 9000-year-old artifacts that archaeologists tried to explain away – like arrowheads or spearheads – because that's right after an epic glacial era. Before, they said, no one, No One, ever lived through a glacial era.

We've been saying,
we've been here longer than 9000 years.

We're beginning to document the dates that show you can live through glacial eras if you have the right landscape, those epic glacial periods that we now know we lived through on this land.

We lived with this landscape and its unique geo-thermal sources. The geo-thermal activity on this land, the geo-thermal cones on Perry's Ridge, the caves and all the other aspects that would allow people to survive through those glacial eras existed here. In other places, they didn't exist and people didn't have the same opportunities to survive.

And I imagine if people survived one epic glacial era, that would have been common knowledge for the next glacial period. Like the Frog Mountain story showed them they were able to survive drought. Where geo-thermal trickles begin and end there are always sedges and little watercresses that grow year-round that are bites and bits of survival.

I know what I know and nobody's going to tell me I don't know because they'd be calling my ancestors liars. I know what I know and you can't convince me otherwise because my ancestors put our knowledge in *captik^{w}łs*.

I hold the wisdom of my ancestors as gospel.

A SETTLER'S REFLECTION:

This story touches on a deep longing in me and a deep sadness. I long to know the layers of history, human history and natural history of this land where I have chosen to make my home. There's so much more here to know than I and other settlers could possibly gather from our brief time here on Earth. Indigenous Peoples have captured and in some places, continue to capture that knowledge through their long connections with different parts of this Earth. Their oral traditions and languages themselves hold so much vital traditional ecological knowledge, about the rhythms and changes, the micro and macrocosms of specific places on this planet.

Relevant knowledge.
Irreplaceable knowledge.
What if we still had all that and more to draw on for our mutual resilience?

And so, when I see how deeply interrupted the Sinixt relationship with this land is, I, we, can only begin to imagine everything that's been lost. Lost to them, yes, but lost to everyone who might choose to love this land, to bond with this *tum xúlaʔxʷ*, to yearn to live respectfully and harmoniously within Earth-time.

We forget that knowledge lost to Indigenous People is knowledge lost to all of humanity.

Indigenous losses are a deep fracture to our evolution as beings embedded in place. But why do we need to be embedded in place, some might ask? Because we are the water we drink, we are the food we eat, we are not isolated beings living only inside and in response to our technologies. We are part of the weather, we are part of the landscape around us. We ignore this at our peril especially in this era of intense climate change.

So I feel grateful for this story, for these Sinixt stories, for these thin threads of mountain knowledge that have managed to survive the devastation of colonialism, exile, disease and genocide. But gratitude is not enough. If this deep knowledge of the Earth and its people is what I really honour, then there's work to be done if we are to staunch the loss of Indigenous knowledge.

K L   K I V I

45

COYOTE AND CHICKADEE

One day *Snk̓lip*, Coyote, met *ćskʕákna?*, Chickadee, heading to the big Council in the sky with his *sumíx* bow. *Snk̓lip* wanted the bow for himself, and so made fun of it. *ćskʕákna?* told *Snk̓lip* to go to the top of the ridge so he could prove how far his arrows could shoot. *ćskʕákna?*'s arrow hit *Snk̓lip* and killed him. *Snk̓lip* came back to life and convinced *ćskʕákna?* to gamble for his bow and arrow, and even his clothes. *Snk̓lip* continued on to the big Council wearing *ćskʕákna?*'s feathers, and came across Prairie Chicken children along the way, whom he tricked and killed. The children's parents were very upset when they found out what happened, and *ćskʕákna?* helped bring the children back to life. To repay the favour, Prairie Chicken tripped *Snk̓lip* over a cliff. As he fell towards the water below, he called to his power to change him into something different. The water bugs helped him survive and he gave them their colour in return.

Story told by Taress Alexis, from *Coyote Stories*.

Art by Chad Thompson

It's a common human thing to covet what other people have, even when you don't understand how to utilize the power of whatever it is you're coveting for good. Coyote is going to the big Council all decked out with Chickadee's *sumíx* bow and arrows, yet he still can't control himself. He could just go as himself and get there and be there, but he has to try and beat those little birds out of their berries; to find mischief somewhere. Coyote wants to have something no one else has. In the end he's doing what he should have done in the first place, heading off to the Council meeting without all these other intrusions. It creates a lot of acrimony not only for himself, but for everybody else he involves and in the whole essence of the story. When he's changing himself, he's thinking *I want to go down*, but he's not thinking any further than that. He's grabbing for things indecisively when wishing to be a pine needle or a leaf.

He doesn't think,
what would be an easier, gentler way to go down?
Forgetting that what he's wishing for
he doesn't even want,
he wishes it away and then back again.

It's a very human thing to do.

There are people in the world who are willing to help out regardless of what they get out of it. They aren't going to the Council meeting; it's not about a competition for them. The water bugs got their colour in return for helping, although they didn't have a big expectation of what they would get from Coyote. Coyote can do good things too, he's not just an idiot. He's a demigod. He is a creator. He can help beings, like the water bugs, in a crucial way that has allowed them to survive for millennia since these creation stories began, a trillion years ago.

Some people are really comfortable with having a *sumíx*, a power, a medicine. Some people come into their power; they know what their medicine is, and they accept their medicine for what it is. It could be something massive, like a grizzly bear. Then you know you have power. But it could be something as little as a tiny bug, and even those bugs have power. If you're comfortable with bug power, bug power is going to be powerful. If you're coveting bear power and you have bug power, you're not going to be that comfortable with it. You're going to try to project something instead of getting comfortable with your *sumíx*, and having that medicine as part of yourself. Coyote covets more power, more *sumíx*, when he hasn't really mastered his own. Lots of people have power and they don't always master it.

**You truly have power when
you master your own *sumíx*,
and you're comfortable in your own skin.**

When you're comfortable with that humble bug power, you aren't coveting bear power. You accept the power you have. If you want bear power, then by all means, go out and search for it. Chickadee had to go out, get that *sumíx* bow, and make it happen for himself. He was the one who was meant to carry it. Coyote covets it and wants it, when he doesn't even have control over his own power. It's that conflict of not being comfortable with who you are and mastering what your power is. Maybe bug power is

stronger than bear power if it's yours and you master it. You can make bug power very powerful, just like little critters.

As Sinixt People, we know about medicine. We understand about medicine. We understand about going after that medicine. When people go out in search of their *sumíx*, they're given a song. They have to sing that song. When they go to Winter Dance, they have to go to the pole and sing their song.

**That is their *sumíx* song.
That song is part of taking care of your power;
it's about acknowledging your power,
and every year you have to go and rejuvenate it.**

When you sing that song, you sing your power up. You sing your luck. You sing sickness away. When people are really strong with their *sumíx* and they go to the pole, their songs just come. And those songs are so strong that when they sing them, everybody dances. When they sing powerfully like that and everybody dances, it rejuvenates their own power.

I've seen other people who go to the pole and can hardly croak out their song. They have to call people in to support them so that they can sing just a little bit. I've witnessed someone that I know covet a contemporary lifestyle that isn't tied to old traditions. They're stuck being Indian, being raised by Indians, and perhaps they want to step away from that. I've seen people who have stepped away and things happen to them because they don't maintain their responsibility. Certain things, like a pipe, when you pick it up, you pick it up for life. You don't get a choice. You don't get to put it down. You can't take that pipe and just give it back. If you do, things happen.

**So when you pick it up
you better make sure you want to walk that road
and you want to walk it for the rest of your life.**

I've seen people who pick up pipes and put them down. They really wanted a pipe for some reason, until they got it. They don't understand once you've made that commitment, it is your commitment for life. To me, it's about being comfortable with your power. What you've got is what you've got, and don't covet any other thing until you know what it is you have. People should make commitments to what they have the capacity to do, and then make a commitment to maintain those capacities. Share as much as you can, do as much as you can. Of course, the first rule of *smum iem* is, take care of yourself first. That's the rule. Feed yourself, feed your babies, feed your grandbabies, put a roof over your head, and take care of yourself. Second rule, be of service.

**Once you've taken care of everything
you're supposed to take care of for yourself,
you have to be of service.
That's a requirement.**

When I chose to be of service I made a commitment to this path. I try to demonstrate beyond a narrow scope of things; being of service isn't just about the Sinixt. Being of service is finding people in your community who are in need. Before it was all about Sinixt, the animals, and the water, because that's all that was here. Now there are people from all over the world here, with many parallels to my own family and what my family experienced. When you see people struggle like that and you know the suffering behind it, if you can, you have to do something. It might be offering money. If I see a need and can address a little piece of it, it's about demonstrating to these community members what I can do. There are people struggling some of my same struggle; how do I lift myself up by lifting them up? Which is exactly what this story isn't about. Hah!

At the beginning of my path, I tried to run as far as I could. But the path led me to all the places I went and all the activist work I did. It was all about learning to walk this path. When you're asked by your elders to do something, you take that on. You have to accept what is your responsibility. If I put it down, as I'd like to do so many times a week, who gets to deal with it? I thought when I was younger if I dealt with it, then my kids wouldn't have to deal with it. Well, my kids do deal with it. If I don't deal with it, then my grandkids will have to deal with it; now my grandkids are dealing with it.

**If I don't deal with this,
I'm not visioning the kind of life
and world I want for my descendants.
I want a world that's already gone.
And I don't think it's coming back anytime soon.
But that doesn't mean we shouldn't vision it.**

A SETTLER'S REFLECTION:

This story impacts me deeply and holds profound medicine. As I was listening to Marilyn's words, I was overwhelmed with emotion around the discussion of power: knowing your own power, being comfortable with who you are, what happens when you aren't. The context of our world leads people to covet power on a global scale that is not aligned with the rest of the human and non-human communities on our planet. I am steeped in a cultural paradigm interwoven with settler colonialism and capitalism, one that presents power as a tool to wield control over others and over life. This encourages the idea that we must step on one another to climb the ladder and get ahead. A world full of people coveting grizzly bear power doesn't leave much room for celebrating the diversity of skills and gifts we each have to bring.

A striking contrast to this modern paradigm is the Sinixt tradition of Winter Dance, a practice that feels very far away from my own lived experience. The depth of interconnectedness that exists when everyone has an opportunity to be witnessed for their unique offerings, and where witnessing others actively feeds and strengthens the community as a whole, resonates in my heart.

The need for constant renewal of our commitments to life is a cultural practice I can tie to my own western European ancestral roots. I know my ancestors also celebrated seasonal shifts and transitions, with the understanding that our relationship to life must be renewed so we remember who we are. My experience of the teaching is that it is both a path to service and a responsibility to continue visioning the world we want for our descendants, drawing on the strength and wisdom of our ancestors as powerful tools for healing.

ALISON CHRISTIE

52

HOW COYOTE MADE THE BLACK MOSS FOOD

Snk̓lip, Coyote, and his son, *Top'kan*, encountered *Nći?cn*, Wolf, in his lodge. As he was butchering Beaver, *Snk̓lip* asked how *Nći?cn* catches beavers and Wolf told him how he did it with a big stick. When *Snk̓lip* tried, he only managed to hit himself with the stick but somehow he caught two beavers who played dead. He tied one to each of *Top'kan's* ears. When *Snk̓lip* was gathering wood to cook the beavers, they ran away with *Top'kan* still attached to them and disappeared down two different holes, thus stretching out his ears. Because of that, coyotes have pointy ears to this day. *Snk̓lip* cut *Top'kan* free. Still hungry, he then saw two *spqmix*, white swans, who he managed to catch. He tied them to *Top'kan* also but when he climbed up a tree to get the pitch top for kindling to cook them, they flew away with *Top'kan*. The *spqmix* dropped *Top'kan*, killing him. *Snk̓lip* jumped from the tree but his long hair got caught and he cut off his hair to free himself. His hair turned into *sq*ʷ*l'ip*, black moss.

Story told by Taress Alexis, from *Coyote Stories*.

Art by Stephanie Kellett

Sqʷl'ip, black moss, is a survival food. It's always there, hanging in the trees, it's always going to be there for consumption. Of course, it's a big process to take care of it, turn it into a food source, but it's important for survival. *Snk̓lip* is such a poor provider because he's always on the edge of starvation so he has to leave something that can be turned into food. Black moss wasn't eaten much and hence a *captikʷł*, a traditional story, was created to remind us of it in case of need. Other foods were much more essential on a regular basis. We honour those foods in our ceremonial feasts.

When we do a ceremonial feast, we always, always serve up ceremonial food in a certain way. Water first, roots second. Then comes berries, fish and red meat. That's considered proper food and proper protocol. After that, you serve whatever – Waldorf salad, fry bread, etc.

I've already spoken a lot about
the importance of water.
It is key to all beings.

The major staple food of the Sinixt People would be roots. It would be the first food you gather in the year. Depending on where you are in the landscape, you would dig *cx̌ʷlúsaʔ*, which is camas, or you'd dig *spiƛ̓m*, which is the bitterroot, first. Right around that time there's also the little *skʷnkʷinms*, wild potatoes, there's wild carrots, there's wild garlic, there's wild celery, there's wild onions and all the lily roots. And they all sort of follow one another depending on where you are on the landscape, which ones would come first, which ones would come second. In that ceremonial food way, the first one dug is the first one served. If you have more than one root, you would serve them up in the order you took them out of the ground.

How you harvest them,
is how you offer them to the People.
That's honouring the roots' protocol.
In that way, roots are a big aspect of our staple diet.

In the olden days, the power bars that were done by the People, were the *cx̌ʷlúsaʔ*. It would have been diced up with dried wild huckleberries or those little wild strawberries and they would have also pounded up some dried elk meat, deer meat, or whatever red meat they had. There would be these little cakes that would be stuck together with tallow – bear fat, elk fat, deer fat – and then formed into little cakes that would easily fit into a pouch or your pocket.

These foods took you across the landscape.

Our second food is berries. Like the roots, there are many kinds of berries: *síyaʔ*, which are saskatoons, huckleberries, thimbleberries, gooseberries, strawberries, wild raspberries, blackberries and *sx̌ʷusm*, which are the soapberries. Even in the huckleberry family there are different huckleberries. If you can imagine one of those treasured, tiny wild strawberries cut down into four or five pieces, that would be about the size of what we call the little people huckleberries. Those are little teensy-weensy huckleberries and if you didn't know what to look for you'd never find them. I find them because of my nose: it smells just like a fair where someone's spinning up cotton candy and that sweetness permeates the air. You'll just walk into a little meadow and that smell will permeate everything and you'll ask yourself, "Oh, what is that?!" You have to lay down and get right next to the earth because little people berries are for the little people. They are so tiny, but so infused with flavour and smell and sweetness and tartness all at the same time.

One of the most cherished trade items is *sx̌ʷusm*, soap berries or soopalallie. *Sx̌ʷusm* is pure vitamin C and detoxifies the liver and the kidneys; it was considered quite a delicacy. There is such a short window of gathering time for the sx̌ʷusm. When it's good, it's magnificent. It's a lot of work though. In Secwepemc Country, they take those 16 ounce tea drink bottles and squeeze the sx̌ʷusm juice out into them and can them.

We don't put a price on those things but we do put a value on them so we can carry out fair trades. As much as there are old stories about Indian People who tried to bilk people with a bad swap (hence the expression, Indian giver), that wasn't our way. We always tried to create equity. Salt itself was a great gift because it wasn't easily available to use for food or for drying food. It had great value.

In terms of the ceremonial foods, then came the fish, any kind of fish, next red meat, any kind of red meat. Even recently, when I was in my thirties, we'd take trips up the Fraser near Lytton with Grandma Mary to go buy wind dried salmon. This old woman would take Grandma Mary out to her salmon shack and ask: "Do you want this kind, or do you want them with no grubs." Even the grubs that were feeding off the wind dried salmon were a prized food for the people. And you'd think, "oh yuck, it's all spoiled now." To us it seems like that but to them it was a real treat. I'm sure those grubs tasted just like squishy salmon gummy worms.

**Everything from fish to birds,
to small critters on the land,
all that is all food.
Very few things aren't food.**

People think we always had elk but elk's a recent thing. We ate deer mostly and caribou since there were huge herds of caribou migrating through here. We ate all kinds of cats: bobcat, cougars. And of course, bear – black bear, brown bear, grizzly. Not all of our people ate bear but some of our people did. The old people said that's how the rumours about Sinixt being cannibals came about. If you skin a bear and don't have the head attached, it looks just like a man, like a human skeleton hanging there. Certain people can eat certain things and certain people are told not to eat certain things. I've never had much of a taste for bear meat myself. My grandma and grandpa used to talk about porcupine meat and how flavorful that was. And beaver and grouse and marmots and groundhogs and those little fool hens.

**Everything was used,
all the internal organs,
everything was utilized.**

As the story says, we never had buffalo but I do believe that up where the Rockies and Columbia Mountains come together there were some mountain bison at one time. So, we'd trade for buffalo meat. I've seen old photos of the people riding back from the prairies, the horses piled high with dried buffalo meat. It was a prized delicacy to have that meat and it speaks also to the fact that the Rockies were our original boundary and of course, people would have done forays to know what's there, to trade and to refine our diets.

In the Frog Mountain Story, Eva said, one of the first things to come up in the spring time that the people ate were mushrooms. We ate everything on the land, everything that had a heartbeat and everything that didn't. We have another anomaly here in this area. We know that there are middens of mussel shells that exist in Kaslo, Argenta and up the Slocan Valley. Those shellfish were so plentiful on these rivers and lakes that where we gathered those mussels, middens of shells developed.

That's the traditional way of
serving up those foods,
being very specific about
how you serve them,
how you gather them.

When I go out to the root fields with my grandkids and I see them out there... they think they're good root diggers but they're not. My granddaughter Celeste will dig a root, pop the skin off and munch it down. When we go home and we're peeling the roots, if we've gotten a little zealous in the field, we'll be up till two in the morning, cleaning those roots. Celeste will sit there with a big pot of honey and these raw, peeled roots and she'll just scoop honey on them and munch them down or eat them plain.

That's an act of resistance,
an act of defiance.
To maintain your culture even in the simplest,
most mundane way,
is to affiliate yourself with a cultural food,
a cultural practice.

Even as pitiful as my family is at carrying out those practices, it is our act of resistance. It is an act of culture, an act of profound cultural practice, because food is so important.

The foods that are on the land and the gathering of these foods is really important to us in terms of being reintroduced to our culture. When you put a root or berry in your mouth and you have that taste, it might not be something you relate to right off the bat but it's something you acquire over a long time. I know it's the same taste my ancient ancestors put in their mouth and tasted. When you talk about that grey matter knowledge, something like DNA but more on a psychological level – basically our deepest understanding or knowing – it is a very infinite universe that goes on and on and on and on and on.

And I know that in my own pitiful way
I'm touching the ancient ones.

A SETTLER'S REFLECTION:

I became curious about local foods from the land as soon as I arrived in the Sinixt *tum xúlaʔxʷ*. I got out plant guide books and began identifying and, if edible, trying out plants and berries. When I heard about Indian ice cream, which is made out of *sx̌ʷusm*, or soopalallie, I was very keen to try it out.

The small, glossy red berries grow on a medium-sized bush with olive-green, furry leaves. They are tantalizingly beautiful. I popped one in my mouth and spit it out almost right away. I'd always been taught that if something tastes bad, it's probably not good to eat. So, I checked with other books and friends and discovered that yes indeed, this incredibly bitter berry is not only edible but sought after by many of BC's Indigenous People.

So, I relaxed my judgment about what "good" tastes like and tried again. The berries were still so bitter that I couldn't eat one without making a bitter-taste face. And yet, there was something flavourful and sweet there as well so I gathered up a bunch and took them home. To make Indian ice cream, you whip up the berries and add lots of sugar, but no matter how much sugar I added, the bitter-taste still overwhelmed me.

I understood then how, much like other Westerners, my taste buds simply had not been developed to appreciate bitterness. As one of the apparently five taste options in our mouths – the others being sweet, salty, sour and now umami (or earthy) – bitterness is taste, neither good nor bad, yet sometimes underdeveloped. Since then, I eat *sx̌ʷusm* whenever I encounter a bush. After over 20 years of eating them, I can now eat two or three without making a face. When I've picked and canned some, I have taken them to the Sinixt Thanksgiving celebration knowing someone there will be able to appreciate them more than I am, thus giving them the honour they deserve.

That said, there are many other native berries that I harvest and appreciate intensely, some obvious ones like huckleberries, raspberries, wild strawberries and *síyaʔ*, saskatoons, others a bit more obscure. It feels good to eat from the land, to link my very body to this place by welcoming its nourishment and to connect with the ancestors in that visceral way.

And now I'm wondering what black moss tastes like....

KL KIVI

COYOTE JUGGLES HIS EYES

Coyote, *Snk̓lip*, came across Chickadee juggling his eyes. *Snk̓lip* tried this out until two ravens snatched his eyes and took them to the Sundance camp. *Snk̓lip* followed them in hopes of getting his eyes back, stumbling blindly along. Bluebird and Bluejay saw him. *Snk̓lip* coaxed Bluebird near and took her eyes but Bluejay replaced Bluebird's eyes with berries. Next, he encountered an old woman, Pheasant, and killed her with a stinging bush and dressed himself in her skin. Bluebird and Bluejay, Pheasant's granddaughter, took *Snk̓lip* disguised as their grandmother to the Sundance where the people were dancing over *Snk̓lip*'s eyes. *Snk̓lip* got his eyes back. Bluebird and Bluejay took their grandmother's skin home and restored Pheasant to life.

Story told by Taress Alexis, from *Coyote Stories*.

Art by Tayler Schenkeveld

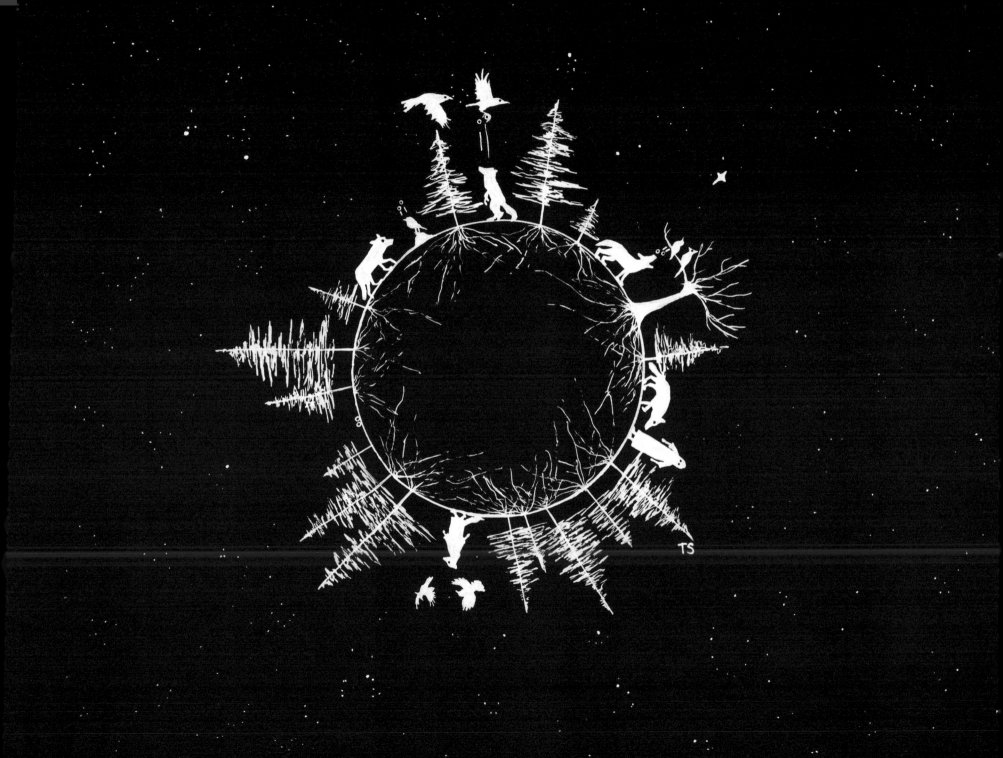

These stories explain how a being is, from ancient times to this very day: a bluebird's small eyes, the arrowhead shape in a salmon's head, a coyote's long ears. There are always associations in the stories with how you experience a creature. They engage our imagination: how would coyote's ears have looked before the beavers were tied to his neck, or the swans pulled him away? What were bluebird's eyes like before coyote took them? Were they bigger, or like some other kind of bird's eyes? I wonder what kind of tail bear had before he lost it ice fishing. We're so limited by what we can see right now, but behind every creature's features, you can imagine there is a story....

Snk̓lip represents the human character. He can be a demigod; he can create great things. He can also be completely destructive and cumbersome. Humanity has the capacity for huge empathy, compassion and acts of kindness for the Earth and for each other in times of trauma. In earthquakes, for example, people are able to act in superhuman ways. On the other hand, there is also the capacity for total ignorance. We can be the worst possible thing for our own selves.

Bluebird is an example of a very naive creature. No matter how much you caution a person who is very naive, their curiosity will cause them to lose their eyes. Yet even when someone gets taken to the cleaners, so to speak, it's often not fatal.

It's critical, but it's not fatal.

Making fun of *Snk̓lip* and stealing isn't a fatal outcome. It's just an outcome. You don't really die from it. But in a spirit way, you die from it. That's why you get to come back to life. You're not really dead, you've just killed your integrity. If you're that naive, you deserve to lose your eyes. Then you get these berries, which aren't that bad, and you can still see the same as you used to. However, if you don't learn and you're still naive, it's not a fatal thing. It's just an aspect of how it is.

That's how life is, we can make really poor choices and it isn't fatal most of the time, but it still marks us.

I think being stepped over three times and coming back to life, having the fog lifted, and clearing a dumb act shows that opportunities for redemption are constantly available. If we continue to engage in those kinds of activities, that's us killing ourselves a little at a time with our own character flaws. Even in the story Pheasant is dead, but not really dead.

I'm sure we can all find examples of times when we ourselves or our friends have been naive. When we try to explain something to them and it's not what they want to hear, they aren't going to hear anything we have to say. It doesn't matter how many times we say it, they're going to believe they are quick enough to get away from *Snk̓lip*, or that it's worth the risk to see that star. We can end up hurt, but in our human nature we're always willing to forgive and go to the next stumbling block.

There will always be characters like *Snk̓lip* who impact others in a profoundly negative way. We have the tendency to forgive, honour and include these characters despite their negative actions, if we don't find ways of maintaining our own integrity. Look at USA politics right now. They just elected someone – Donald Trump – whose actions impact others in a profoundly negative way, and honoured him with a position of power. To me, this speaks of a human condition that's been around a long, long time, back to these *captik*ʷ*ɬ* stories.

The reality is that when you look at life, characters come and go, evolve and devolve through your existence. You can't surround yourself with only certain kinds of people that can be easily tolerated and not have to experience those who are frustrating and infuriating when they come across our paths.

**Those people are there for purposes
and some of those purposes are for us
to learn levels of tolerance.**

It doesn't mean we tolerate what they are, or what they represent, but we do end up learning to tolerate their behaviour because it is there.

**The real lesson is in our ability to
create space around bad behaviours that exist.**

They're always going to exist. If they didn't exist, and we only had to tolerate what was good in our lives, we wouldn't learn patience, we wouldn't learn humility, we wouldn't learn empathy. I think today, the scales are tipped in terms of bad behaviour, and it shows what we have turned away from is the result of not having stories to address it. In the past, these stories functioned to address bad behaviour through example. It was not an option to create an apathetic mindset or state of being where you can decide you didn't want to deal with something and pretend it no longer existed. Those people are a part of our communities.

**If you don't deal with bad behaviour,
you're in some way condoning or colluding with it.
You are actually creating a substantial flux to
the behaviour which impacts many,
many more times than it would
if you just dealt with it.**

If People of Colour weren't pushed to the Civil Rights movement, there would still be white people behaving the way they did towards Black people before there was a Civil Rights movement. Of course the Civil Rights movement had to have people who stood up and said, I'm not going to the back of the bus. It had to have the Martin Luther Kings and the Black Panthers, the more "radical" aspects of change. People are still calling for that with Black Lives Matter. It didn't change everything that it should have, and I'm not saying everything is good with Black people in the world because obviously it's not. But levels of tolerance for that behaviour went way down when it was actually voiced to others, when the behaviour was owned and people said you can't do that, you can't behave that way. Did it stop the KKK? No, but it stopped the open brutality of that level of racism that existed in society.

**People don't change unless
they're challenged to change.**

When you get to the place of extinction, it's about non-natives, non-Indians, non-Sinixt people taking action. It's not about us. What I've always said about privilege is it takes somebody who has all of those perks and amenities in their lives, who holds the power, to wake up and recognize their foot is on somebody's throat. When they wake up, look down, and realize they are stepping on someone, they're going to say, oh my god, how did that happen?! If they move their foot slowly off the throat and see their privileges crumble, for example see a loss of wages because there's a growing equality in wages, they begin to lose some of that power previously held. Chances are, they're going to put their foot back down. It's like *Snk̓lip* going around being a jerk because he can. Because he's living the privilege.

**It takes a lot of consciousness to
actually pick your foot up,
take it off of somebody's throat,
put it down, and suffer the consequences.**

White supporters of the Civil Rights movement who were beaten, some of whom lost their lives, took their foot off the throat and said I'll suffer the consequences. And they did. That's what it takes.

**These stories are about
responding.**

Learning tolerance, yes, that's one aspect. We do have to learn tolerance but we also have to address the bad behaviour. One of the ways we did that was by talking about it in stories, actually seeing an example, and opening the door for others to address bad behaviour. Or, for them to learn the tolerance needed so they didn't go out and kill the person they couldn't tolerate!

A SETTLER'S REFLECTION:

This story reminds me that humans, with our free will, have the ability to both create and destroy, to both heal trauma and inflict trauma. The more the choices to destroy and to inflict trauma are accepted without consequence, the more that type of behaviour proliferates within our inner worlds, and within the external world. Steeped in colonialism, capitalism, and the patriarchy, I exist in a society where the negative aspects of free will are normalized. Tolerance means holding space for ourselves and others in which to learn from mistakes by being held accountable. By holding a space of tolerance, and by responding instead of reacting, learning and forgiveness are possible. Tolerance does not mean ignoring destructive behaviour. Responding does not mean taking a punitive stance and declaring oneself or the other beyond redemption.

I have been sober now for almost seven years. I grew up in an environment where everyone turned a blind eye to the addiction and mental health issues in our family. Throughout my twenties I unconsciously surrounded myself with those who would tolerate the destructive choices I was making because of my addiction. This created fertile grounds for the destruction and trauma to proliferate. In the end, it was spirit that held me accountable, offering me the space in which to learn to make loving choices. As my choices shifted, so did the quality of my community environment.

As a settler, I can learn tolerance for my own ignorance of colonization, as well as the ignorance of others, by starting where I am, educating myself about the history of the community in which I live, and responding with engaged action. I believe we can begin to hold the negative impacts of large-scale bad behaviour accountable by creating safe spaces in which healing can occur. These spaces must include the voices of Indigenous People, the voices of spirit, of our diverse ancestors, and of the natural world. The lack of intimacy between humans and the non-human world is the trigger finger of the empire. By entering into dialogue with the non-human world, through ritual and ceremony, and by taking action based on the solutions that emerge, we can move towards redemption. Help is always available.

RHONEIL OLHA EURCHUK-LUHOWY

WHY MOSQUITOES BITE PEOPLE

There were five brothers, the youngest of which was Mosquito, *Slaqs*. They fed him blood from their hunting expeditions. He was the only one of his brothers that hadn't received his *sumíx*, his power, so he slept in the sweat lodge one night. That night, enemies came and killed his brothers, but *Slaqs* escaped by tricking them. *Slaqs* built a canoe and cried for his brothers as he floated down the river. As he sung his stuttering death song for his brothers, he got invited by various villages to come to shore and eat. He refused until one village offered him uncooked blood, which he accepted. The villagers set his canoe loose on the river. In *Slaqs*'s haste to capture his canoe, he fell on a stick and all the blood flowed out. A small fly flew out and began to sing *Slaqs*'s stuttering song. This fly will sing the song for the dead and live on the blood of humans as *Slaqs*'s revenge for the death of his brothers.

Story told by Taress Alexis, from *Coyote Stories*.

Art by Kiala Löytömäki

Slaqs goes on a journey as a result of his brothers' deaths. That journey involves honouring them and because he honours them as hunters, the only food he accepts to eat is blood. His choice symbolizes the most basic thing – the blood of life. Only certain things can feed your need, your spirit, your quest for meaning in life. In memory of his hunter brothers who supplied him with raw blood, *Slaqs* continues to eat only blood to this very day.

A recent case in the BC courts in Nelson (autumn 2016) was to establish Sinixt hunting rights in Canada, where Sinixt People currently have no rights as Indigenous People. The Desautel Case is about hunting rights. Yet, do the Métis have to establish their presence anywhere in Canada? Hell, no. Do they have to be tied to a home base? Hell, no. If you have a status card, you can hunt as long as you're on a reservation. The Desautel Case is not recognition of Sinixt People or their autonomy. It's about hunting rights in this *tum xúlaʔxʷ*. It's not recognition for Sinixt People, it's recognition that we do exist somewhere and you can hunt here because this *used to be* your People's traditional land. It does not challenge our extinction.

The case also did not acknowledge what has already been set in place by the Sinixt people who have been working in the Canadian part of our *tum xúlaʔxʷ* for over 30 years. Over the years, what we've worked out with the Conservation Department about Sinixt protocol for hunting here in our *tum xúlaʔxʷ* are the following:

**The current protocol for hunting
in the Sinixt *tum xúlaʔxʷ*,**

**is that first,
you ask permission from
Marilyn James or Taress Alexis
as the matriarchs of the Sinixt *tum xúlaʔxʷ*.**

**The second protocol is
that you share the meat that you hunt.**

To have good hunting luck, you need to be generous. Keeping all the meat for yourself means you can get stingy, the animals can get stingy, the land can get stingy. If you don't know who to share the meat with, you can bring it to the head woman. We're not taking the meat and filling up our freezer – we know people who need food. That's part of our process as *smum iem* too, and what helps us take care of our community. So if people come in and ask permission to hunt, then we have meat for those who need it. If we receive anything, we always pass on a certain amount of it to the community, or even all of it. We'll share up what we have for fundraisers also, because people are donating their time for baking and cooking and it's not fair to ask them to dig into their own pockets for supplies. Part of our commitment in this protocol, is that whatever comes – wild meat, fish – we share. That's how we've established this protocol and continue to maintain it on this landscape.

When you know who's coming around to hunt, then you can also establish who knows how to hunt. You can guide them in some direction as to what areas were hunted out and where they might find animals. It's also a protocol to what animals are being harvested from the landscape. Understanding and knowing how those harvests are being conducted on the landscape is part of how we maintain our responsibility.

My advice to people around roadkill, is that if roadkill is fresh, then I think it's fine. The problem with roadkill is you never know how long the animal has been lying on the road, even if the body is semi-warm. It takes a long time for a living animal's body heat to diminish. So, you could touch it and say – oh, it's still warm – but it could have serious internal injuries, its intestines blown out on the inside, and that would taint meat. I've been given roadkill by people before that I was reluctant to feed even to my dogs. I think that unless you've witnessed the animal being killed or you know it's happened within minutes, it's not a good idea.

When an animal holds blood in its body, that's trauma meat – the blood doesn't spill out. That's why you bleed out a lot of animals. You can't expect to consume trauma meat and have happy thoughts. You can't wait a long time before you gut an animal. All those internal organs have to come out so that they don't have time to spew any toxins into the meat. That's why you gut a carcass right away. If that's what people want to eat and they're comfortable with eating it, that's fine but it's not an appropriate gift to Sinixt People or to elder people.

Meat is a sacred thing.
Meat is a sacred thing.
Meat is a sacred thing.

Not all hunters know how to take care of their meat. The way we were raised, you'd never open a package and find a hair on your meat. It was not allowed. Any place where the meat was discoloured, it was all trimmed, cut away. So you got the finest cuts, no dirt, no hair, very professionally processed.

Because I grew up with brothers who went hunting with my Dad, I was not really allowed to know what's done at the hunt. So the initial hunting practices are not my forté because none of that was done at home. None of the guts came home. That stuff is critical. You don't kill pregnant does, you don't kill bucks in rutting season, certain kinds of practices, you just don't do. We skinned the animal at home so I know how to take the hide off an animal. Knowing how to cut it up and process it, oh yeah, that we did, but none of the initial stuff at the site of the hunt.

The practices around hunting honour
the fact that every living thing
gave a piece of itself
so we could be created.

Eva told me a story of how the Sinixt People came to be. The critters, she said, were always fussing and fighting and nobody could establish the kind of leadership or reverence that needed to happen for everything they wanted. So they decided a new being needed to be created. Every living thing gave a piece of itself so that we could be created.

Although that just smacks of Darwinism to me – and I can't stand that idea of Darwinism – my partner David offered me some new perspectives on those ideas. He explained that you have to understand that it's religion. One party against another party against another party. But, he said, if you listen to Indian People or other Third World oppressed people around the globe talk about religion and spirituality, it's very much like these stories; it's moralistic in some aspects of the story, but it's not preachy. It's not: here's the point and if you don't get my point, you are going to hell. Looking at spirituality in that aspect, it's the same idea around Darwinism and white people's perspective around creation. He said, maybe some aspect of Darwinism is there – maybe the dolphins could talk to the whales could talk to the wolves – there was a universal species language and things happened in a really hybrid manner in the evolution of the world and all of it's species.

But it's hard to think outside of those boxes because of that patterning, of imprinting of colonial ideas. Instead, trying to look with a different lens and trying to clear away the colonial fog – what's wrong with certain aspects of those evolution theories? Nothing. And we laughed about it because David said, "I'd rather have evolved from a monkey than a man."

**And, according to Eva,
everything gave us a piece of itself.
That also speaks to the fact
that we have memory of this landscape
even before we were people.**

We have grey-matter memory. When our DNA is passed down through our lineage, we actually have some imprinted memory in our brains that follows those lines of descent. Often, I'm told

what to do from somewhere beyond me. I don't necessarily know what I'm doing when I'm doing it. I don't have that prior knowledge. But I know what I'm told what to do. That's coming from somewhere, that isn't just pretend. When I go back and search through my memory banks, to figure out – what did I actually say? I can remember the actions but I'm pretty much told to mind my own damn business in terms of what did my ancestors say, what did my ancestors do.

**Some things we can know
and some things we can't know.**

Some things we think we might know, but the ultimate, ultimate, ultimate purpose is not to pretend. Don't pretend you know. If you're just a tool, you're just a tool. You can't expect to be the person working the tool if you're just the tool. You've got to appreciate that at least you have some part in the scheme of things, even if you're just the damn wrench and you're there for that quarter turn. That's still a part of the function of how it works.

A SETTLER'S REFLECTION:

This past summer I was challenged by the mosquito, nearly driven mad with the incessant buzzing and itching caused by this little creature. I often found myself asking the question: why do mosquitoes bite?

In this story, mosquitoes are said to eat the blood of humans in order to remember the dead. In my own selfishness, I wonder how long this mourning will last. Is it fair for the generations who have come after those who killed *Slaqs*'s brothers to atone for acts they did not themselves commit? Yet I remind myself: I have no idea of *Slaqs*'s suffering. I cannot know how long his healing process must last. The process may take generations: the memory runs deep.

The story emphasizes the importance of initiation: the rites of passage that mark the transition from child to adult states, from which we can draw power, meaning, and purpose in our lives. It is common to hear the question asked (often with mock despair): what is the purpose of a mosquito? Deconstructing this question, however, reveals embedded colonial attitudes. In the dominant culture, if something does not have a clear and immediate "use" it is often considered disposable. (For example, common roadside "weeds", which are in fact sacred medicinal plants).

I realized my own acceptance of Darwinism is deeply embedded, and through this story it was challenged. The theory of evolution, promoted as elegant and benevolent in the school system, has been used to help justify the persecution and subjugation of many races, based on the view that Europeans are the 'fittest' race. Far from simply being a 19th century notion, this mutation of Darwinism is still pervasive in public discourse and decision-making: consider underlying reasons for the neglect at investigating the thousands of missing and murdered Indigenous women, or the response to the current opioid crisis.

In my reflection, I attempt to have empathy for the mosquito. They need blood to live. We all need the blood of life. Perhaps we can think of this as part of their purpose: to help us remember we need to give a little so that others can live. To remember what we have lost, what has come before us, and that – whichever religion or theory you believe in – we all came from the same place. Does it help the itch to go away? Not really. But it does help me appreciate the perspective that there is meaning in all things, and that all life is precious and none is more valuable than another.

FLETCHER FITZGIBBON

CRITTERS HELP THE HELPLESS

This is a story of a physically challenged man and woman who grew up in a village where they participated joyfully in all work. They were well loved and honoured in their community, particularly by the children. Eventually the man and woman got together but they were childless for a long time. After many years, they had a son they loved so much, they spoiled him. As he grew, he became lazy and demanding. They sent him away to another village to learn how to survive. There he met a woman and they came back to be married in his parents' village. It turned out he had chosen a lazy woman. She had a child and around the same time the old man died. Because the family was *ṁpaʔpaʔsílx*, in their year of mourning, the village took care of the family. When the villagers went into the mountains for annual gathering, her son and family abandon the old woman there without food, heat and shelter for the winter. A packrat and a mouse helped her survive the winter. In the spring, the warriors went to see what had happened to her with her son following behind. The warriors were very angry with the son but he pleaded with his mother to be spared. His mother took him home.

Story told by Marilyn James

Art by Rhoneil Olha Eurchuk-Luhowy

When I tell this story, kids get upset.

The son should have gotten a spanking and why didn't he get a spanking?

They really believed he should have gotten a spanking. If his mother would have allowed them to spank him, they would have had to spank her too. He got to be that way because someone wasn't responsible. She allowed it, she taught him, she brought him up that way. If he got a spanking for being that way, then she should have gotten a spanking for bringing him up that way.

Sometimes you find your allies among the most humble, and they're not what other people would think are the most impressive beings to be standing next to. A lot of people might have judged the fact that she was crippled, as not being physically whole, or a high functioning being, or a beautiful being, since that's how they look at people who have challenges.

Sometimes you find your allies among the most humble.

Her alliances were with those creatures who are seen as lesser beings. Sometimes the not so impressive allies – a mouse, a packrat - can respond to your needs in a way that is impressive. It might not be more than you need or as much as you think you might need to survive, but it's those little allies that get you through. And being grateful for those little things that get you through, is impressive. What's more impressive to have as a *sumíx*, a whale? A wolf? A grizzly? Or a mouse?

Teaching kids how to be responsible is crucial.

Comparatively, how I was brought up and how children are brought up today, I can see the children of today don't know how to respond if you ask them to assist you. When I was a kid, if you were asked to do something, you knew you better respond. It got you thinking about the request itself and whether you were getting something out of it in return, when you are asked to do something,

When I talk to schoolkids today, I tell them, this is your job, going to school is your job. What do you think the roof over your head costs? What do you think your monthly food bill is? What do you think those tennis shoes on your feet cost? What do you think those clothes you are wearing cost? This is your job and you're getting something for it. Your job is to learn. Go to school, learn and conduct your responsibility to educate yourself. You might have other jobs too, like chores.

In order for your existence to get better you have to participate in it. For you to survive in a good way, you must participate.

This is how to create valuing instead of devaluing; this is how to create aspirations to get better, to know better, to do better. There are always lazy jerks who want someone else to produce for them. Those who have an air of entitlement, and because they might be more pretty or more whole than somebody else, they think society owes them something. It becomes a very fine line to walk between love and responsibility, responsibility for how you bring somebody up.

It's my responsibility to speak up about the Sinixt. Where my limits are, soft or hard, it doesn't matter anymore. That's when you have a commitment. You have a hard line. When you tell the truth and don't sugar coat it and make it all sweet.

That's my responsibility.

Especially when what needs to be talked about is relevant to my People, is relevant to this land, is relevant to this water, relevant to all of it, I have a responsibility.

No settler person, no expert, no author, no tribal government representative, no CEO of a mining company or Columbia Basin Trust or CPC or BC Hydro or Fortis, or the Ministry of Forests or the Ministry of Environment or.... whatever can tell me what I can talk about or not talk about in public. All of a sudden someone who thinks they are important, might think they know what's more important to the Sinixt than I do, and tell me how I should address my issues in public, what I should talk about or not talk about in public. The only person qualified to decide what I talk about is ME. To tell the truth - that's my job.

It's <u>my</u> job to provide a Sinixt perspective.

If that's being manipulated or being disallowed, you're missing a severely important aspect of what a Sinixt person like myself would offer in terms of our laws, our responsibilities and what we would like to see preserved on this landscape.

If we don't have a say,
and if we don't speak out,
then colonial oppression is being layered on us
again and again and again.

The silencing that's happened and continues to happen is highly insidious and deep. It's complex and there's a whole swath of privilege walking around here making a lot of CEO dollars, a lot of consultant dollars, and getting corporate recognition, ministerial recognition, institutional recognition and oppressing Sinixt representation out of the picture.

So, like the mother who raised her son in a certain way, settlers haven't been taught or they haven't necessarily translated what is required of them into their behaviour. If we, as Sinixt People, have the requirement to behave a certain way on the land, then we should have the same requirement of settlers. If we have a requirement to be responsible to our community and community members – to be of service – then we should have the same expectations from the settler population that is here. Unfortunately there are a lot of settlers who feel those rules don't apply to them because they're Indian protocols, and they don't feel like they have to live up to them since they do things differently. When, in reality, there are a lot of ways to do things with a level of respect, with a certain amount of knowledge. You don't just come in and make rules willy-nilly as you go along, and expect to be accepted by everyone in the community, to be treated the same way by everybody. I think those standards need to be equalized and we need to have the same levels of expectation for everyone here.

**For your existence to get better,
you have to participate in it.**

A SETTLER'S REFLECTION:

Hearing this story, I too wanted the son to be "spanked." How could he abandon his mother like that with no consequences? And yet, her response shows us what the deeper levels of responsibility are in a community. It brings up for me what it means to ally with someone and to ally with the Sinixt in particular, because I wasn't the one who displaced the Sinixt, yet I'm here.

What is my response-ability, my ability to respond to the extinction of the Sinixt, to the fact that their perspectives and voices are ignored and dismissed by settler institutions and individuals? How do I, as a settler, step up to this situation with a level of historical understanding and respect? How do I grapple with the knowledge that I do and don't have?

It's easy to think – *I need to be a cougar and jump in with teeth and claws bared* – spank that bad guy! But what if that isn't what's called for? What if that isn't my way? What if, like the old woman in the story, my power comes from something small and persistent like a squirrel? What does my work look like in this situation then?

I think we disempower ourselves frequently these days, telling ourselves we're not the ones who did the harm or we have nothing to offer because the issues seem so huge and insurmountable. When actually, our work is nothing more than to speak the truth as we see it, in the way that we were gifted to do so. For a musician, this might mean a song. For a writer this might mean a story. For someone who likes to interact with their neighbours it might be bringing up topics that need to be aired. For someone else, that might mean donating money. For yet another, it might mean making a meal for someone in need. There are as many responses as there are people and my job is to figure out what it is that I have to offer.

What is my responsibility? Sometimes it's easier to think we have no responsibilities and nothing to offer but it's my experience that it's more fulfilling to step up and step in.

KL KIVI

LEMON CREEK

The Lemon Creek archaeological site has been studied for many years, by many generations of archaeologists, including Dr. Nathan Goodale, Alissa Nauman, Dr. Anne Prentice and Dr. Ian Kite. All of these archaeologists have consulted with Sinixt elders including Alvina Lum and Eva Orr. These elders were the original consults to Dr. Kite and Dr. Prentice. Starting out as a student at the site, Dr. Goodale is now the Professor with Hamilton College out of New York State, and the lead archaeologist at the Lemon Creek site. He utilized the next generation of Sinixt elders including Marilyn James and Bob Campbell as consultants, thus the consultation over at Lemon Creek has followed two generations of Sinixt People as well as two generations of academics who joined the project. At this site, they discovered the largest and oldest pit house in North America which is carbon dated, give or take a few thousand years, to 9,000-12,500 years ago.

Story told by Marilyn James

Art by Amber Santos

MOURNING DOVE
circa 1915

NAVA
circa 2016

EVA ORR
circa 1990

MATTIE
circa 1850

MARILYN JAMES
circa 1990

MATTIE
circa 1850

Ella Fry-McClung
circa 1842

NAVA
circa 2016

MATTIE
circa 1850

Ella Fry-McClung
circa 1842

NAVA
circa 2016

MATTIE
circa 850

NAVA
circa 2016

MOURNING DOVE
circa 1915

MARILYN JAMES
circa 1910

Ella Fry-McClung
circa 1842

When archaeologists study the Sinixt People and come up with the artifacts, and date them at 9,000 years old, they say, this can't be. This can't be the true history of the land, because the Sinixt only existed here 9,000 years ago. They didn't just come into existence and make spears and arrowheads.

**As Sinixt People, we're saying,
that's because we were here longer than that.**

The whole idea that we've existed on this landscape for 12,500 years, through three epic glacial periods, to us only speaks of the land itself. It speaks of what the land has to offer and the relationship Sinixt People have had with unique facets of this landscape. The thermal cones that exist here would have created pockets of survival in extremely cold conditions. Incredibly ancient, ancient fish, like the *ʕayckst*, the bull trout that we're named after, are beings that have existed on the planet through many epic climate eras. The survival of those ancient beings here, as a food source, having a relationship with the land for that long, also speaks to the Sinixt footprint on this landscape. I think archaeologists just assumed because this landscape had epic glacial events no one would have survived here, and that it wasn't worth looking any deeper. It's really an incredible aspect of our story, that archaeologists keep having to roll back time and say there's something phenomenal about the length of human existence on this landscape for the periods of time we're talking about. It's highly reflective of our relationship with this unique landscape itself.

All of these villages that exist, these pit houses, these subterranean dwellings we lived in, were adaptive architecture. The pit house depressions that you see all through here, in Vallican, point to a long series of occupation. People think these villages were only here once, and the people didn't exist here after that, but these villages have been occupied over thousands of years. In some pit house sites there are layers of occupations that flow over long periods of time. These villages existed in flux, the pits being used and reused, disused and reoccupied. They are permanent winter structures.

At the Vallican site, there would have been several of these pits occupied by families, as well as some single person units and two person units. A pit house as big as the structure we have rebuilt there would have housed maybe four families. When you look at how small this village might seem but at the occupation of those structures, you see there is a large basis. Where the pit houses are bigger, more people who lived in smaller pit houses would have joined families in larger structures.

**People were always coming to
community to participate in
whatever was happening.
Participation is key.**

The young fellas would have been off with their bows and arrows or slingshots, maybe looking for rabbits or wild birds to put in the stew pot. As the snow was very deep here, they may have been able to go to places on the landscape on top of the snow, where they could reach some of the dried branches. Wood was a huge gift and a great commodity that everyone needed.

The more wood, the more heat from a fire pit. The kids knew how prized even little sticks were and what bringing wood to warm up a place would mean to the people living in those pit houses. People went out to get some air, to play and to the river for water. This was also about assessing the landscape: where you went, how things were.

There would have been a sweat lodge everyday in the morning. The sweat lodges were done separately, with males in one and females in another lodge. If they were using the same lodge, they would have been held at different times. People would have finished their prayers in the morning, their sweat lodges, and come together as a village to tell stories, perhaps have visitors, or in the winter, just visit among themselves.

People didn't stay in their winter dwellings, the pit houses, all year long. As soon as the snow would break up and the roots were coming up somewhere, they would leave. Those gatherers would get their stuff together and go off as a group. One faction of the village would head out, with hunters going in another direction. The gathering would happen for different items in different places.

The kind of *cx̌ʷlúsaʔ* I dig grows way south, whereas other people, who dug the purple kind of *cx̌ʷlúsaʔ*, would have dug around here if they couldn't do that kind of travelling. It's a long ways to walk from here to Castlegar, and to those big fields up on Indian Point, but not as far as the Colville Rez in Washington. The fields are up above Brilliant, called Indian Flats.

When the people left in the summer, sometimes they didn't come back the following winter. Perhaps they'd be gone a couple of winters, or at least one, and then return to the village. They would account for all the people they visited. There would be multiple inquiries about the land and the water here, what was happening there. Their experiences were educational for the community; where and how they gathered food, who they met up with, what other events took place. As things came to more recent times, that would have included settler encounters, and sicknesses. It was a report of who was still living, who had died, what the chief or headman was doing over there, who the head woman was that saw to everything in another community. All the old gals would want to know, how did they treat you? If they treated you well, you had to gift them.

It's like that.
It's a storytelling,
a witnessing,
because people are interested in everything.

There might be baskets to show, new weaving techniques, new copper pots, a new man, a new woman. That's what these villages would have done this time of year, in the winter. It would have been a big social gathering. Of course, Winter Dance was only a month and a half past and people were still talking about it. Winter Dances are spiritual practices for renewing our songs, and fulfilling our relationship with those songs and our *sumíx*. It is also our commitment to our foods and our land. It happened over winter solstice, usually a four-day event that included singing songs and dancing. It was called a jump dance, a Winter Dance.

I've seen some really large pit houses and I know one on the west side of the Slocan River is very large, so maybe at that carbon-dated time, one structure represented the entire village. There's more structures on this side, but that particular structure is the only one that's carbon-dated. There are occupations on both sides of the river because the rivers were our highways. Where the river narrows in that spot, it would have been a good fishing site. At Lemon Creek you've got all kinds of fresh water river highways. You can travel quickly when you get on those rivers and if you know what you're doing and you can handle a canoe.

If you observe the landscape now and what's on the landscape, such as the trees, it's nothing like it used to be. You can look around in the pit houses here and see huge trees growing out of the centre of the pits. Obviously those trees weren't there before. Another example is, we have tonnes of snow this year. At this time last year you could see patches of ground. The landscape and our perspectives of the landscape are always changing. There were once pit houses everywhere where settler's houses are now. At Lemon Creek, they're only studying the pits down by the river because those are the ones that are left. All the other places were plowed under by former or current settlers. Many of those historical sites are gone, no longer there. You can't even fathom how huge those village outlays would have been, occupied over long periods of time. Of course there's many archaeological studies being done at different sites, all finding the same sort of carbon dates on them. Eleven hundred, two, four and five thousand years: all those different dates connected to this landscape.

Our existence has been so extricated from the landscape, we can never know the extent, because of the attack on those sites on the land.

Even now, there is a lack of knowledge about sites that haven't been carbon-dated, where they're at and if they're protected or not. According to legislation they're supposed to be but that doesn't mean anything to a lot of people.

A SETTLER'S REFLECTION:

As a settler anthropologist, I'm aware of how settlers look to the science of Archaeology because of a disbelief in Indigenous elders. Archaeology is used to verify traditional knowledge passed down over generations. As settlers we think science has validity, forgetting how much science has changed over time and was sparked by Indigenous oral traditions. This perspective also downplays the importance of knowledge-keepers in Indigenous cultures passing down the "history" of their People. I struggle for a better word than "history" because it denotes written records and the culture-bound assumptions they contain are more accurate and reliable than oral records. In the end, elders are usually not surprised by what is found, because they have known it all along. They are just waiting for science to catch up. It is their stories that make these sites come alive, that puts flesh on the objects unearthed in the archaeological excavations and help archaeologists to make sense of what is found. Artifacts are pieces of a puzzle, but it is the elders who hold the picture on the missing puzzle box, as this story clearly demonstrates.

Destruction of archaeological sites - unfortunately more common than excavation - is an attempt to obliterate Sinixt presence. As settlers, there is a struggle to create a narrative that justifies our existence in someone else's territory. How can I own land, when there is no treaty in place? According to the *Royal Proclamation* of 1763 a treaty must be signed in order for lands to be alienated from First Nations. There is no treaty here. Sinixt aren't even recognized in that process.

Meanwhile, other Indigenous groups, in the deeply flawed and colonial land claims process, contribute to the attempts to obliterate Sinixt from this landscape. This is the on-going process of neo-colonialism where Indigenous Peoples are pitted against each other in hopes of getting a fraction of their unceded land back—this is the work of colonialism. Here too archaeology plays a role, the scientific evidence as to whose territory this is.

The involvement of Sinixt at the Slocan Narrows Archaeology site is a crucial piece of understanding the puzzle pieces. The work of Goodale and Nauman represents the potential of truly collaborative archaeology.

LORI BARKLEY

CHICKADEE MAKES A *SUMÍX* BOW

This is the tale of Chickadee, ćskʕáknaʔ, who, on his way to the big Council in the sky, made his sumíx bow of Elk's rib. To do so, ćskʕáknaʔ had to first cut sník̓ɫćaʔ's, Elk's, throat as he crossed the river on his back. Once reaching the other side of the river, sník̓ɫćaʔ dropped to the ground, dead. Mother Wolf appeared and tried to trick ćskʕáknaʔ out of his meat by sending him on a mission to bring back her wolf cubs, who were in a basket near the trail. ćskʕáknaʔ was wise to the attempted trickery, moving the basket further down the trail and telling Mother Wolf he could not find her children. When she went to look for them, ćskʕáknaʔ climbed up to a ridge to roast and dry his meat, and make his sumíx bow. Mother Wolf returned with her cubs and asked ćskʕáknaʔ to send down some meat for them, but instead he dropped a red hot rock wrapped in fat down each of their throats, killing them. He then resumed the task of making his sumíx bow from sník̓ɫćaʔ's rib.

Told by Taress Alexis, from Coyote Stories.

Art by Amélie Blanchard

**In the Sinixt version,
everybody is the way they are supposed to be.**

This is a story of power, what motivates us to seek it, how we navigate its acquisition in relation to others, and what we do once we have it. If you want real power, in some ways you have to be, or appear to be, very ruthless. And in the old ways if you were given a task, you had to do what it took to carry it out. Back then it was a lot rougher. You had to go through a lot, it was brutal, and that was part of survival. So if you had to kill mother wolf and her babies to get to the big Council, then that's what it would take. There is a distinction between trying to take something of someone else's that has power and following through with your creator-given task of finding your own power.

**You have a responsibility to your path
and the part you play in the whole.**

There are obstacles and setbacks that will inevitably present themselves as you follow this path. If you achieve what you go after, do you have the capacity to hang on to it? Do you have the capacity to use it for good? How do you direct it, because if it is a power, it means it has to be directed at someone or for someone. It takes on those moralistic questions of: who has the power? How do they use it? How is it perceived to be brutal? And if you want power, again, there's a price to be paid. There is a brutality about it.

In terms of *sumíx*, which is your spirit power, it always requires some kind of commitment to attain that. It takes some effort.

And you have to be up to the task of those efforts.

**In the Sinixt version,
everybody is the way they are supposed to be.**

So it's not who's wrong, who's right; who's the good guy, who's the bad guy. Everybody has the capacity to be a real jerk one moment and stellar the next. We all have the capacity to be dumb as hell, and then the next minute, have real intelligence because within another realm we have some intelligence. Within that realm we have some capacity. In another realm, we might just be total no-capacity idiots.

**I look back at my capacity for knowledge
and my capacity for thinking through my colonial fog...**

What are the morals here? We all have these capacities, we all have these lack of capacities. The best example you can have is a really good example of a bad example. If you're given those examples you can say - *oh man, I'd never be that kind of idiot* - and then turn around and be that kind of idiot.

There are always the people who are there to take advantage of whatever anybody else has. Chickadee killed the elk. It was chickadee's meat. As soon as Mother Wolf showed up, Chickadee knew there was going to be some trickery involved. You can almost predict that anytime you have something someone else wants, they will come along and tell you a story or give you a line. They will try to trick you out of it in some way and make it seem like they're helping you, or they're going to benefit you in some way when in reality, they're going benefit themselves.

In the Sinixt version,
everybody is the way they are supposed to be.

Killing and greedy behaviour are tendencies that are characteristic of all human beings, actions necessary to defend the sacred, to maintain our *sumíx*, our source of inner power and medicine. There's many gullible people in the world and at some point you can count on yourself being gullible in one realm. You're only gullible until you're intelligent enough not to be gullible in that realm.

It's the con,
it's the big con.

Don't go out looking for something that isn't yours to have, don't go out looking to con anybody. If some mother came to you and said, here watch my kids, that's like immediate established trust. You shouldn't be trusting that easily. I'd look at somebody and say, are you nuts? I don't even know you or your kids. What levels of trust do you appear to be demonstrating to somebody else? Letting somebody think that you trust them, and trying to establish that trust immediately, that's a big con.

I think if the Wolf had asked, "could you share your meat with me?" it might have been a different scenario. But instead of being upfront about it, the Wolf got embroiled in this sort of trickery, the hustle. Don't fall for the hustle.

Even when the hustle's over,
don't fall for the hustle.
Even when you've got the upper hand,
don't fall for the hustle-
you know it's the hustle.
And I think that's a really serious problem
in humanity.
I think so many people swallow hook, line and sinker,
the con.

Because we want everybody to be nice. We want everybody to be truthful.

And what is the con's face these days?
Corporations.
What is the con's face these days?
Politicians.
What is the con's face these days?
If you're a person of colour, cops.
You can say the cons are here for our benefit. For whose benefit? For what benefit? It's **their** benefit, it has nothing to do with the people that they're supposed to be benefiting. That's the con.

Many of these people, to this very day, are jeopardizing the lives of their children by dirtying the water, creating militaristic systems and committing hate all over the world to be reflected back on our own beings. If you're willing to sacrifice your own children, that's the biggest con and it's horrifying...

Don't fall for the hustle.

A SETTLER'S REFLECTION:

I struggle with this story; I want there to be more clearly defined sanctions of good and bad behaviour. I was taught to define justice as punitive, retributive punishment for hurting someone else to get what you want.

**In the Sinixt version,
everybody is the way they are supposed to be.**

To believe that there will always be the face of the con artist, the hustler, the character leading us astray through trickery requires a lens of acceptance that is not available through the Western narrative of understanding morals in storytelling. I want evil to be brought down, and good to prevail. But what happens when good and evil are options that exist within each being; when one character personifies multiple and seemingly incongruent capacities?

**It's not who's wrong, who's right;
who's the good guy, who's the bad guy.
Everybody has the capacity to be
a real jerk one moment and stellar the next.**

If this is true, then it means sometimes I take what I want from the world at the expense of others, sometimes I play tricks to get what I want. But I don't like this, because the narratives in my life have taught me I must only be good to be accepted, and all my negative qualities must be rejected.

**I look back at my capacity for knowledge
and my capacity for thinking through
my colonial fog...**

I realize that I feel and experience this story through a colonial fog; one that simultaneously denies and perpetuates evil...

It's the big con.

And whilst denying I could possibly embody the qualities of trickery, I myself can become the face of the con. The face of the ones unable to embrace a full range of human qualities and tendencies – attached to my ego and unwilling to acknowledge my part in the hustle. I myself become a target for the hustle by looking away from seeing its true nature; from this place I am rendered unable to access my own power, my own medicine. Am I willing to let my own greedy tendencies and behaviour die to maintain the integrity of my inner power and medicine?

Don't fall for the hustle.

ALISON CHRISTIE

COYOTE QUARRELS WITH MOLE

Snk̓lip, Coyote, his wife Mole and their children were living away from the other people one winter, and they were very poor. Each day Mole would go out to gather herbs and moss to keep their five children from starving; she also carried all the wood and water. One day Deer offered a fawn to Mole, and she sent her children to bring *Snk̓lip* to kill the fawn. *Snk̓lip* missed the fawn with his arrows. They quarreled and *Snk̓lip* tried to kill Mole, who tricked him and got away. *Snk̓lip* could not take care of the five children on his own, so sent them to their uncle Kingfisher, except for the smallest boy. They went travelling together, and he came across Mole in disguise. He tried to kill her again, and again she escaped. He gathered his son and they went to find new lands where his tricks were not known.

Story told by Taress Alexis from *Coyote Stories*.

Art by Hannah DeBoer-Smith

In most of the stories there's a matrilineal thread in terms of the children. *Snklip* has a favourite son, a favourite child, and that always comes with a hardship to the rest of the family. Or it's just accepted as the way it is. He'll go off with his favourite child and then Mole is left to care for the rest of the babies and the family. I think that speaks to why we were a matriarchal people: there isn't a lot of male responsibility in terms of family. This is not to say that there isn't male wisdom passed down.

**The mothers and the grandmothers
hold the tribes and the families together.
They are the glue.**

Snklip sees no urgency in his family being hungry, or in his role to provide for them. There's nothing about him that provides for his family. Even at the moment when he could very easily, he provokes ineptness. Men are supposed to be hunters, protectors. They're explorers, members of the community who go to check things out. They knew the territory, they were observers of the landscape and what was going on. They were the fishermen and learned it at a very early age. They were providers. If they went out and got a big piece of meat, they brought it back to the village; it wasn't theirs. It belonged to the women. The women took care of it, dispersed it among the families.

Even in our ceremonies, in our way, men and women don't sweat together. You can use the same sweat lodge but you would never be involved in that ceremony together. It's a different energy, and it's important to recognize and separate that on every level. It's not to say that men don't have a place because they do. But I think in our contemporary brains we try to figure out what men are supposed to do, how they're supposed to be, and we have this expectation of them that can't be fulfilled.

**Everything here belonged to the women.
That's what smum iem is.
The role of the mothers and the grandmothers
is very important.
There are protocol after protocol
around women practising being women.**

There are moontime protocols. In the olden days which isn't practical these days, women went to a moon lodge. In other words, when she began her menstrual cycle, other women would pick up her responsbilities, feed her man, feed her children, take on her responsibilities in the community. A woman would retire to a moon lodge and that's where she would spend time observing the protocols around isolation.

They didn't isolate themselves from other women, they isolated themselves from their responsibilities. During this time, you didn't pick medicine, you didn't pick berries, you didn't touch meat, you didn't prepare food. You just didn't do those things. It's not practical in contemporary times but there are ways you can address some of those issues. Women would help other women carry that. If a woman was in a moon lodge, other women would bring her food either from the community pot or from her own fire. And, women on their menses will draw other women and then you might have a whole village of women in the moon lodge at the same time. Who'd be left in the village to care for everyone was the women who no longer bleed. When a woman gets to menses, and she begins her moontime life construct, which is the construct for birthing.

Babies were rejoiced.
Babies were to be babies,
human being gifts to the village
through a woman.
Everyone in that village had that baby.

Babies fulfilled the next generation responsibilities of women. You weren't allowed to birth year after year after year. A baby had a responsibility to be a baby and deliver that baby gift to the village for quite some time. Each woman would only give birth every 5-7 years. She would withhold having another birth for that long. Then she would feel, at that time, if she wanted to birth again. That speaks to a plethora of psychological issues people have today about mssing their childhoods, feeling they didn't get the love they needed. When you're the baby and you're treated like the baby for seven years, you get what you need because you're held to that structure of babies.

You start learning all the serious stuff about life and then you step into another role, as a child, then finally as an adult. Back then, adulthood began as soon as you produce the kinds of things the community needed. Most children by the age of 11-13 were considered adults. They could do most things adults could do but they were encouraged to pick up those skills

Another thing this story speaks to is a cultural practice of

when you can't provide for your children, they can go to other members of your family who have a greater capacity. There always seems to be one that gets kept, or is raised by the parents who couldn't raise everybody and generally it's the oldest of the group. This story depicts that kind of custom adoption by family members except it's the youngest who's kept, not the oldest four. And someone who can't provide knows they can put their responsibility on other members of their family who have the capacity to do so. So the four older brothers of Coyote and Mole go to Uncle Kingfisher. Usually the person who has that capacity to make it work for everyone, to feed the kids, and to provide is also able to embrace bigger responsibilities. They know they can do it, it's not a challenge: it just is.

There's a view in Western culture of someone expecting you to give or contribute as a hardship. In some ways it may be an honour. My mom was custom adopted by her uncle and his wife. She knew who her mother was but her mother didn't raise her. They adopted two more kids that were relatives. When I take care of my nieces and nephews, I feel honoured to step in and take on that responsibility, and for their trust of me with their children.

This is what our traditions are:
if there's some way you can give
in a positive way, you're obligated to do that.
That's the path I followed to come home.

A SETTLER'S REFLECTION:

Even as I began to listen to Coyote Quarrels with Mole I immediately felt aware of how little context I had for the story. I do not know the conditions in which it was told. Though I have heard one or two, I do not remember any of the other Sinixt stories about Coyote and have heard none about Mole. I know so little of the culture in which this story is situated.

I am left grappling in an ocean of my own settler interpretations. Upon reaching the end of the story I feel sadness. How did Coyote come to be this way? So void of empathy, blind to the needs of his family, prioritizing only his own whims? Had he always been this way?

And Mole – how did she become married to this man? Did she once love him? Does she still, despite his awful behaviour? What happens when she tells him how she is affected by his negligence? And their youngest son. What will become of him with only Coyote now to model kindness, generosity and responsibility?

I also found myself wondering in general about how the Sinixt have and do conceive of gender and gender roles. I admit that I tend to feel very wary when I perceive rigidity in people's beliefs about gender roles. There seem to be so many exceptions to any rule we could make about how all "men" are and how all "women" are. And yet, I have never lived in an intact culture that has tested its conception of gender and gender roles over millennia. I feel curious about whether strongly defined genders and gender roles might feel truer to me, were I to experience them as part of the intact culture in which they were formed and in which I, and those around me, belonged.

SAMUEL STEVENSON

98

CHIPMUNK AND OWL WOMAN

Chipmunk, *q̓ʷq̓ʷcwíyaʔ*, was picking saskatoon berries, *síyaʔ*. Owl Woman, *Snínaʔ*, tried to trick her into coming down to add her to her basket of children to eat. When *q̓ʷq̓ʷcwíyaʔ*. jumped over *Snínaʔ*, the Owl reached up and clawed her, leaving stripes down her back, but she got away. When *q̓ʷq̓ʷcwíyaʔ* arrived home, her grandmother tried various ways to hide her and protect her from *Snínaʔ*. Meadowlark told grandmother where she could hide *q̓ʷq̓ʷcwíyaʔ* and grandmother offered her a gift to keep her quiet. *Snínaʔ* couldn't find *q̓ʷq̓ʷcwíyaʔ* but Meadowlark gave away her hiding place for a price. *Snínaʔ* ate *q̓ʷq̓ʷcwíyaʔ*'s heart but grandmother brought her back to life. *Snínaʔ* and *Snk̓lip* met and decided to make a fire to roast the children in her basket. They let the children out to gather wood for the fire and when the fire was roaring, *Snk̓lip* and *Snínaʔ* danced together. *Snk̓lip* pushed *Snínaʔ* into the fire where she perished.

Story told by Taress Alexis, based on *Coyote Stories*.

Art by Tannis Wood

Coyote uses ceremony in this story to trap *Snína?* Though he's responding to her treachery with his own, he does it to save the children she's planning on eating. Coyote reflects two aspects of humanity in this moment: both his capacity for virtue, by working to save the children; but also his treachery, which is equally an aspect of being human. It's important to remember we all, as humans, have these capacities. Coyote calls his ceremony a "Sundance" and it might have aspects of that original ceremony, but he's basically just using it, and flattery, to lull her.

If we talk about the Sundance that's mentioned in this story and others, it's one of the many ceremonies that have been on this landscape that aren't here anymore. To believe that there was a Sundance on this landscape at one time isn't hard to fathom. Even though today what we see as Sundance is related to the Lakota/Dakota/Nakota tribes out in the Plains - Plains Indians style - where it is associated with fasting and praying and those aspects, we also practiced Sundance. And many times, our ceremonies also included those things.

**Our ceremonies have, of course,
evolved, devolved, re-evolved,
devolved and re-evolved
over millienia.**

Not only did we have a Sundance, we also used to have a Medicine Wheel. When people think of concepts of Medicine Wheel, they can't think of it in terms of today's ceremonies. I revert back to the teachings of my elders, now my ancestors. In terms of the reburial of our ancestors, for example, we don't have a concept of the ceremonies, the burial practices that put our ancient ancestors in the ground 1000 years ago, 3000 years ago, 10,000 years ago. We would be very disrespectful to lay a contemporary ceremony over someone who was buried with those ancient ways and practices. When we think about these ceremonies, our conceptual vision, our conceptual reality cannot bring to light the traversing of practices over those long periods of time. When it comes to ceremony, there is an evolutionary and devolutionary process that happens that doesn't transcend millennia. It has its space in time in which it exists and then it doesn't.

**I know that we have many ceremonies
that don't exist anymore,
like the Medicine Wheel.**

We have white people trying to bring that ceremony back. To me, that is the ultimate disrespect. To think in your contemporary mind that you could conjure up a ceremony that has existed on this land and disappeared, when the people who actually practised it don't have a clue of what that consisted of, is disrespectful.

I know one thing about the Medicine Wheel ceremony – just one. When my people used to practice Medicine Wheel, Eva Orr said they carried the stone that they would stand upon during the ceremony and placed it in the Medicine Wheel. There were no cars, so you didn't throw a big stone that you were going to stand on in the trunk of a car and zoom off to the site. That meant you had to physically carry a stone, then stand on the stone for probably four days and four nights – feasting, sweating beforehand, sweating during, sweating afterward – while standing on a stone that you physically carried there. I know that much; the people trying to resurrect the ceremony don't even know that much. And I know I know nothing.

One of the things that Eva Orr asked me many years ago was if I could try to bring the *Stx̌àɬq*, Huckleberry, Ceremony back.

I agonized - how am I going to do this? Eva's asked me something I have no concept of. How can she ask me to bring a Huckleberry Ceremony back? She gave me only minute clues: that only women were present; there was a flat bench of land up the Slocan Valley where it was practiced; that it happened during huckleberry season; that there was a dance. Now for me to go and bring back a ceremony, that's a huge task. I wouldn't want to pretend and make things up, I would want to know what the hell I'm doing. I don't want to be disrespectful. I don't want to be pretending and just make something up, like so many ceremonies conducted by people who know absolutely nothing about the culture they're appropriating from.

I was, of course, a lot younger when she asked me, so I thought: when am I going to start getting clues? When's it going to happen? Now I'm getting geezerly and I'm not going to climb the mountains in the Slocan Valley and find that spot. Now, my perspective is that when the right woman granddaughter, great granddaughter, some non-relative but someone in the future, some Sinixt woman descendant in the future – shows up, she will have a dream, she will have a vision, she will have a GPS in her that will take her right to the land.

What I anguished about was "oh, it was all about me", but in fact it wasn't about me at all, it was a piece of information. It was a request given to me to carry forward, to keep the visual perspective alive in someone's head, so that someone in the future would know, "hey there was a Huckleberry Ceremony. I bet you I know where that spot is. I'm going to go up there and see if there are huckleberries." Of course the landscape is not going to be anything like it used to be, but the important part is keeping cultural perspectives alive, just like these stories.

These stories are about keeping cultural perspectives alive.

Do we understand every little bit of it? No. It is our job to know the stories, to hear the stories and to think about the stories. We might have a concept and as soon as we have it, throw it aside. As these concepts grow and the reasons and rationales of truth begin to ring, it's like having a tuning fork that's off, with an edge to it, and then all of a sudden, it has a hum. When the tuning fork has reached its fine tune to reality, then a truth, a fullness, a feeling, of emotion of concept that we're supposed to evolve around emerges.

Vision questing is also a very important aspect of Sinixt cultural existence.

Knowing, presence. It obviously played a big part in how we brought our children to their own *sumíx* and their power. Little children went out on vision quests, even five-year-olds, like my granddaughter Nava. Her perspective of a mountain wouldn't be the same as mine, but again it's her perspective we're playing with. So we might take her up a small hill, tell her she might have to stay there. We would give her a couple of rocks that spark and tell her she must hit the rocks together during the night and show a spark. That proves she is there, that proves she is following her quest. We would tell her that something might come to her and then she gets her *sumíx*, her spirit power. She might get a song. She might be taken by something. Like Eva – she said that she was taken by eagles and kept for three days. She was just a little bitty thing and when they found her she had crusty blood around her mouth because the eagles had fed her.

And of course, we live in contemporary times and child protective services become a very active aspect of our lives and especially since they target Indian parents. If we were to take our children out and leave them out on the mountains for three days, four days at a time with no food and no water, you can bet that we, as parents, would be punished. Within our cultural practices, we would be following full-on what vision questing is all about. The older you go to vision quest, the harder it is to achieve the goals – that's my perspective. Vision quest has a place. I've vision quested myself and received many gifts.

You don't have to vision quest to get a vision.

If you know the difference between a vision and a dream, you can have a vision in your sleep. If you are skookum enough, you can actually attain dimensional shift, fully wide awake, not drug induced, just make a dynamic dimensional shift fully conscious. I've done that before too. Being open isn't about a certain dogma, a certain practice, a certain door you go through to create this openness.

The doorway is you,
the openness is you,
if you give yourself the space
to create those realities,
those dimensional shifts.

Sometimes I've gone out and fasted with no food and with no water for four days. Some people say, "that's life threatening, if you do that you could die!" But I know better than that. You're not going to die from no food and no water for four days, but you're going to be damn thirsty and damn hungry. You're certainly going to be picturing what you're going to eat and drink for the last two days but that's how your mind works. If you leave the visions of drinking lemonade and eating watermelon behind and you enter into that doorway of hunger and thirst that is huge. If you embrace it, you begin realizing how certain privileges hold you back.

Certain privileges retard you.
Certain privileges,
like having your belly full every single day,
make you less grateful for the food you consume.

When you can drink water anytime you want and you also have the choice of soda, or wine or whatever, you find yourself jonesing for other things when they are accessible. You stop appreciating what a pure, cold clear glass of water is to a body system that is completely devoid of hydration. There are huge limits to having access to things.

There are many aspects to vision questing that create those doorways for us to reevaluate who we are as a people. How we appreciate things. Where our gratitude is. You also become really small in the world – you're a little ant in the ant hill of the world. You see how little of a player you are as a human being in this world.

**Whatever importance you seek is
nothing unless you hook your anchor
to something bigger in terms of a continuity of existence,
a continuity of knowledge and knowing.**

I think as human beings we have certainly devolved, not evolved. We may have evolved in certain ways – we can drive cars now, we have computers and telephones – oh, we're so evolved! We're super devolved as human beings knowing and understanding our place in the world and knowing how to exist. We don't know to look at who we are as we exist and who is around us as we exist.

Art by Axel McGown

A SETTLER'S REFLECTION:

When owl woman, *Snína?* , is introduced to the story with a basket of stolen children, it immediately makes me think of Canada's tragic history of removing/stealing Indigenous children from their homes. Colonial Christian beliefs of "right and wrong" became the dominant narrative while they, the colonial authorities, hypocritically and systematically abused children. Communities were left childless. The practice of removing Indigenous children from their homes due to cultural differences continues today through child protective services.

When chipmunk, *q̓ʷq̓ʷcwíya?*, leaves home to pick berries in the forest she is confronted with the danger of being stolen, and possibly eaten (death). Although she escapes the owl's claws that tore her fur they leave their mark on the generations of chipmunks to follow. I think about the impact of colonization on generations of Indigenous families, the pain and sadness of this loss.

In the Sinixt reflection, Marilyn speaks about ceremony, and children going on vision quests. She says that vision quests can provide many gifts, including a sense of gratitude and/or your spirit power. These practices help one evolve and better understand their place in the world.

It makes me feel sad that people were forced, incarcerated, even killed for practising beliefs that have the intention of creating more connection and gratitude in the world. Perhaps if settlers had respected these practices, or even had their own that serve these intentions, there would be less oppression and exploitation of the things that serve to sustain us.

I really like that *q̓ʷq̓ʷcwíya?* is revived. I think about resistance and resilience. There is a death, but also a rebirth. A re-creation of what was lost. The Sinixt reflection speaks about devolution and evolution, a process that is fluid not dogmatic. However, evolution (growth) isn't painless. With such great losses comes great responsibility as noted in the reflection. One cannot just recreate these processes thoughtlessly, as white people have tried to do by appropriating bits and pieces of cultures.

Like many stories cross-culturally, there is a moral to the story. *Snína?* perishing in the fire is her paying for the evil workings of her mind. A reminder that at some point we are held accountable for who we are.

STEPHANIE MEITZ

106

TAKWIYA

There once was a village by a river with many children. On a hot day, the children were playing by the river while the adults worked. It was so hot they fell asleep on the beach. One of the little boys awoke as it turned to evening, and panicked as he remembered the story his parents told him about Takwiya, with her long fingernails and bad breath. Takwiya would come to the village at night and take the children away who were out at night and eat them. None of the others were concerned, but the little boy hid in the forest. Then Takwiya appeared, gathered up the children and took them home to cook them. The little boy was able to save his friends by pushing Takwiya into the fire, where she exploded into mosquitoes. That is why, to this day, mosquitoes go after children more than adults.

Story told by Taress Alexis, from Coast Salish tradition

Art by Devon Ecru

I first heard this story told by an acquaintance of my mom and dad's at a storytelling festival. We used to go every year to these gatherings of traditional oral storytellers from all over the Northwest. There were usually some workshops, but the first night was the best because they would always have a great opening. A man named Ed told this story and he would have the whole audience falling off their seats because he got so into it. When he did the breath and the long nails part, everybody got into it. That's where I got those actions from, and I always remember him telling that story, his face; he was even sweating a little bit. He was short and round and had these big cheeks, a long scraggly beard, smiling eyes and was wearing a suit jacket. It instantly became one of my favourite stories.

In community, a lot of us tell our kids - *don't go out after dark*. I think parents used these kind of stories to teach children there's a relationship between the darkness and when it's appropriate for a kid to be outside playing. Besides it being a spooky story, it's teaching about behaviour. There is also the importance of where the story takes place. The baskets and shells in the story are important cultural symbols.

If you look at aspects of collective human behaviour, there can be a mob mentality where everybody gets on board and goes down a path that isn't a good path to be on.

In the story, there is the boy who was awake and saw something no one else was seeing. There's always someone (or perhaps many people) with a little sense and a different way of looking at things that helps the survival of the many. That person is paying enough attention to see when something goes wrong. Although they may still be part of the collective action doing the wrong thing, they remain conscious it could go very wrong. The story isn't speaking to an ultimate hero who was there to save the day from the beginning. That person was really running with the crowd the whole time. But he was the only one who listened to grandma!

This continues to be a human dilemma, even today. When we were growing up, there were people who dissed the cultural perspective of stories. They would say – *Oh those old people don't know anything, we don't need to listen to that, it's a new day.* But there are the kids who do pay attention, who are proud to know what they know, and who are asking the questions and being respectful enough to sit there and listen while other kids run out the door to play. The ones who listen will say things like - Granny is there something you want? Is there something I can do? That's a traditional way of being brought up around that kind of knowledge. I see it with my grandkids; there are the ones who want to know, and the ones who would rather watch TV than listen to grandma's stories. They are the sparks.

We need those sparks to counter the density of evilness, of dimness, of low intellect. Huge players like Nelson Mandela, David Sohappy, Alice Walker, Abu Lord in Syria, David Monogye,

Bill Wappepa, Reverend Tutu, Mother Teresa, Dalai Lama, are chosen. People who demonstrate some control, compassion, peace and love are necessary. Or big warriors. On the other side, it's not light and love – and that's what these stories are about also – the other side. It's about the Hitlers, it's about the Trumps, it's about the evilness that permeates the world and its existence as well.

You might not have a lot of respect for some people, but you don't show them disrespect. If you disrespect them by interrupting when they speak or ignoring them, that's a reflection of yourself. There's purposeful, meaningful and very direct ways of challenging people you don't respect without compromising your integrity. I'm strong enough to stand up to the people I don't have respect for and I'm willing to show my community and family what I think and feel openly. They can make up their own minds.

**It's highly courageous to teach children
to listen to the stories of their elders,
and also to challenge someone who is a leader
if you don't believe in them.**

In terms of creation stories, creatures could have once been something else in former states of being. They transform and are now in another state of being that isn't anything like the original. If you believe the scientists, a chicken could have been a velociraptor. Although we may find chickens quite annoying, and not the most beautiful creatures around, they're nothing like what a velociraptor probably was. In the same way, we may find mosquitoes quite annoying, but they are nothing like Takwiya! These stories explain evolution as a process of moving through existence. Insignificant things can become fatal things. Some insignificant seeming creatures can do great deeds, like the frog saving the People. We as human beings may have always existed as *homo sapiens*, but we've evolved as human beings nonetheless. Even if we existed in this human form 12,000 years ago, we're completely different now. Culturally, environmentally, we exist in a different climate. My ancestors lived through two glacial eras. Today, we couldn't even imagine how we might exist through that without massive technology, 60-degree-below-zero sleeping bags, and all the trappings. Our People have, and our existence is something that has travelled through the evolutionary process on this landscape alone.

**We're not the same form we once were;
we're always evolving.
What exists here now isn't exactly
the same as when it started out.
That is the transformative nature of existence.**

A SETTLER'S REFLECTION:

The legends are true. That's what sticks out for me hearing this story within a story. As with every one of these stories, they are not based in fantasy but in our world. They may provide entertainment but they are also leaving us with layers of messages about how to be in relationship with ourselves, with each other, and with the land. Takwiya gives us even more: it is a glimpse at how we relate to stories.

It's so easy to be one of the children on the beach, in disbelief of Takwiya being more than a spooky tale. I've definitely been the person to doubt and say, "It's just a story, go back to sleep" or to betray my intuition with the thought "It's just a feeling. I'll ignore it." Maybe you've been in that place, too.

The Western scientific model is one way that we cast doubt on anything that can't be evidenced or reasoned. I often have to remind myself that Western science is a colonial framework, and it's only one way of seeing the world. For those of us raised within this context, the idea of knowledge being transmitted through an oral tradition seems simple and unsophisticated.

It takes a lot of unlearning and reframing for me to see that these stories are anything but simple. They are complex and contextual, embedded with generations of insight and teachings. In Takwiya, through the belief and bravery of a little boy, we see the importance of stories and the wisdom they hold, wisdom that is only valuable when we choose to listen.

A story is never just a story. In some sense or another, all of the legends are true.

AXEL MCGOWN

COYOTE AND BUFFALO

This is the story of why there are no buffalo along *Snx̌ʷntkʷitkʷ*, the Columbia River. Of course, it's Coyote -*Snk̓lip*'s - fault. When *Snk̓lip* went to the prairies and found the skull of his enemy, *Qʷspíćaʔ*, big bull Buffalo, he treated his remains disrespectfully. *Qʷspíćaʔ* came back to life to avenge this disrespect. *Snk̓lip* tricked *Qʷspíćaʔ* to not kill him by helping *Qʷspíćaʔ* win his herd back. To thank him, the big bull gave *Snk̓lip* a buffalo woman as long as he agreed not to kill her and eat her. However, *Snk̓lip* killed and ate her so he went back to get another Buffalo Cow. When *Qʷspíćaʔ* gave the Cow the choice to go or not, she refused. *Snk̓lip* returned to his country without buffalo forevermore.

Story told by Marilyn James, based on *Coyote Stories*.

Art by Christie Van der Burg

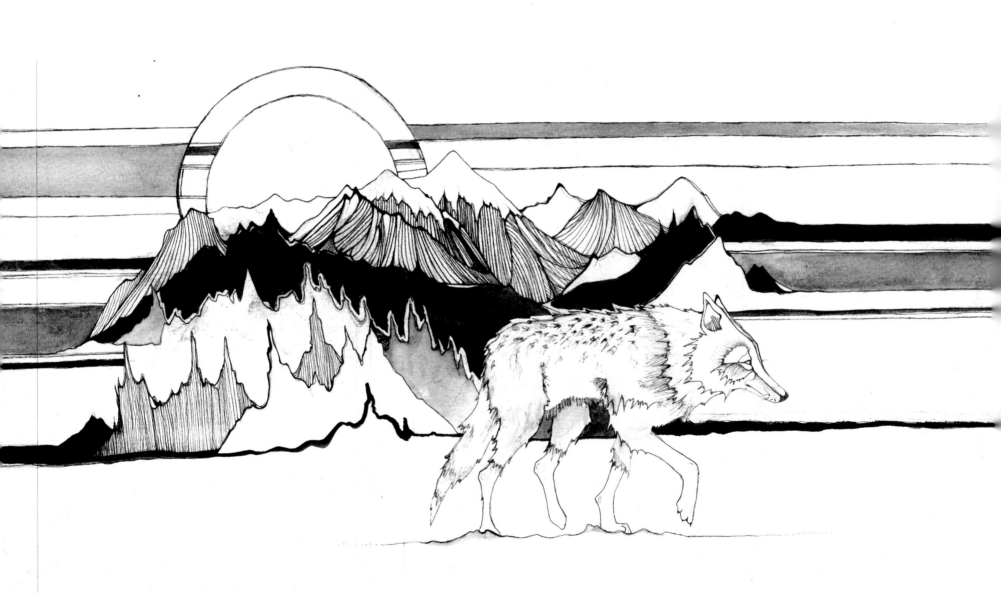

Ancestors aren't dead.
They're living still.
They're a part of life, still.

Our People had a much more solid connection with the spirit world and how we're living in these dimensional shifts in our very existence. The bones of *Qʷspíćaʔ* are not just objects, they are aspects of creation on many levels, some unseen. That's also why we don't pick up our artifacts and take them away because our ancestors are still using them. We realize that we might not have the eyeballs to see them using artifacts but that doesn't make it right for us to gather them because we're limited in our ability to see into other realms.

This story is about learning to respect the dead.
This story is about how not to disrespect the dead.
The dead need respect like everyone else.
You don't disrespect the dead, you just don't do it.
This story is about how we learn to respect the dead.
It is.

When Coyote kicks and curses the Buffalo's skull, he demonstrates disrespect. Sometimes, the best example is a bad example. Or a bad example is the best example of what not to do. Coyote is good at that. *Hee hee.*

It's never okay to dig up anybody's buried ancestors, it's never okay to disrespect anyone's burial grounds, you give these things a wide berth. We were taught to treat everyone's ancestral remains with respect. Our return to this area in the late 1980s

was precisely for this reason. The process of road building in Vallican was unearthing layers of old graves at our village site there. Our ancestors' bones were being excavated and taken to museums in violation of all our laws. This desecration gave birth to the whole reburial movement in Canada. We were the first People in Canada to successfully negotiate the return of our ancestral remains. To date, we have recovered over 60 ancestral remains and reburied them where they belong. (See Repatriation of Remains story.)

Critical to our cultural practices as Sinixt People are the protocols around *ṁpaʔpaʔsílx*, around death. *ṁpaʔpaʔsílx* is the time of grief, when someone close to you dies. You follow protocols. You don't touch anything. You don't participate in ceremony; you might be there quietly, you might witness and observe. You don't hunt, you don't fish, you don't gather. You don't do anything because that has dire consequences for everybody. When you touch and gather plants, or hunt and fish, you're putting grief and death on that food. During *ṁpaʔpaʔsílx* our communities knew to take care of each other. In the past, that was possible.

If you gather plants,
you're putting grief and death on that food.
If you hunt
you're putting grief and death on that food.
If you fish,
you're putting grief and death on that food.

Today, it's not possible to fully observe *ṁpaʔpaʔsílx*. In our contemporary history with the arrival of settlers, we experienced the five great dyings – the delivery of the smallpox blankets and the great dyings where 50% of the population of villages were lost. When so many die, there isn't anyone who isn't *ṁpaʔpaʔsílx*. There was no one to take care of you and see to your needs and bring you fish, no one to bring you food, bring you roots, bring you berries. Everybody had to go out and put death on the land. You had to eat death, you had to share death, it was everywhere.

**Everybody had to go out
and put death on the land in order to survive.**

Death on the land.
Death in the air.
Death in the water.
It was hard, everybody had to eat death,
drink death, breathe death.
Death was everywhere.
Everybody was *ṁpaʔpaʔsílx*.
Think about it, everybody... everywhere...

The purpose of *ṁpaʔpaʔsílx* is similar to leaving a field fallow, so when you go in to re-sow your seeds, to create a new or similar kind of field of crops, it produces much better. Because you let the ground rest, you let yourself rest. It's taking the time to feel those emotions, to observe them. Why wouldn't you be sad, why shouldn't you be sad? A lot of our People cut off a finger so they would always remember... there would be something missing, and when they went about their daily business, they would remember... oh, yeah, I no longer have that part of me.

We all die.
Nobody gets out of that scene.
We all die. It touches us all.

m̓paʔpaʔsílx gives children an opportunity to understand that aspect of their very own life, of what they're going to have to deal with in their life. We need to give ourselves licence to understand death and come to terms with it. When you're feeling a little pushed in terms of *m̓paʔpaʔsílx*, our practice of taking it to the water is a good way to lighten the load a bit. You talk to the water and tell the water exactly what you're feeling. Take it to the water and tell the water about your experiences of grief. Ask the water to help take that away.

Grief is a shared experience. It's about all the people who don't have that person in their life anymore. It's about all the people with the varied experiences who come together and make that person whole in their experience. The person who died doesn't have the same relationship and the same experience with every single person. We each have a facet. Grieving together lets us recreate that person and their whole life experience with each of us bringing our little sliver to become part of the whole. That creates an holistic expression of grief for how we grieve and how we need to do that collectively. If you only grieve your piece, you're not really honouring or praising that person in the way that they should be held up.

The way they should be held up.
The Way They Should Be Held Up.
Held Up to be Honoured. Ancestors aren't dead.
They're living still.
They're still a part of our lives.

A SETTLER'S REFLECTION:

The finger. After I wrote out my initial reflections about this story and discussion, expressing how wonderful and acknowledging Sinixt grieving practices were, I was left with the finger.

For me, the work of decolonization involves searching out the things I refuse to or cannot see initially. It was one sentence in Marilyn's discussion, just one word actually, that disturbed me: why make a big deal of it? But it is precisely because I was having these rationalizing conversations with myself that I knew I needed to look deeper. Then the finger showed up one night, when I awoke from a dream and couldn't get back to sleep again. The truth of the finger sat down on me and insisted I look.

When the Sinixt were grieving the loss of a close family member, a person sometimes cut off their own finger. Cut off their own finger. A living symbol of loss. I do understand the symbol, the external representation of deep inner pain, of loss. When my father died, I felt like I'd lost a huge and vital part of myself, a pillar of my psyche, I'd say. I loved him and honoured him deeply and observed my own version of *ṁpaʔpaʔsílx* in grieving his death. Talking about Sinixt traditional grieving practices with my friends helped me express my own needs and reality in my time of mourning. It's a stretch to picture a community where people take care of a family's needs for an entire year, yet it's possible.

But a finger?

What the removal of a finger evokes for me is a sense of interconnection among family, among community, that I can barely imagine. Raised in the colonial me/mine-you/yours paradigm, I perceive body parts as sacredly my own. "Us" ends at the airspace around my skin. Is this the colonial fog Marilyn alludes to in her discussions? The place where we fail to imagine, to comprehend, that family can be woven so tightly together that the loss of a parent, a sibling, a child, a spouse, can merit the removal of a finger? That's a huge decision to make.

A few weeks later, I came across a reference to the young men of my own People (Mulk/Estonian) cutting off a finger, the trigger finger to be precise, to avoid being drafted into the Tsar's colonial army. An act not of grief, but of self preservation, of resistance. Big moments require big responses.

KL KIVI

RATTLESNAKE AND SALMON

Ntytyix, Salmon, marries a beautiful woman and brings her home to the big falls by *Snx̌ʷntkʷitkʷ*, the Columbia River. *x̌aʔx̌ʔúlaʔx̌ʷ*, Rattlesnake, kills *Ntytyix* with an arrow. Three wolf brothers take *Ntytyix*'s wife home. *Ntytyix*'s body is carried until it washes up just as a skull and backbone. Mouse restores his life and *Ntytyix* returns home to the falls. *Ntytyix* burns *x̌aʔx̌ʔúlaʔx̌ʷ*'s house down and *x̌aʔx̌ʔúlaʔx̌ʷ* dies. When a small snake crawls from *x̌aʔx̌ʔúlaʔx̌ʷ*'s eye, *Ntytyix* condemns it to always crawling on its belly. *Ntytyix* then takes his wife back and exiles the wolf brothers to the forest and that is how timber wolves came to be. The arrow point that killed him remains in his head and every salmon has an arrow point in their heads to this day.

Story told by Taress Alexis from *Coyote Stories*.

Art by Coleman Webb

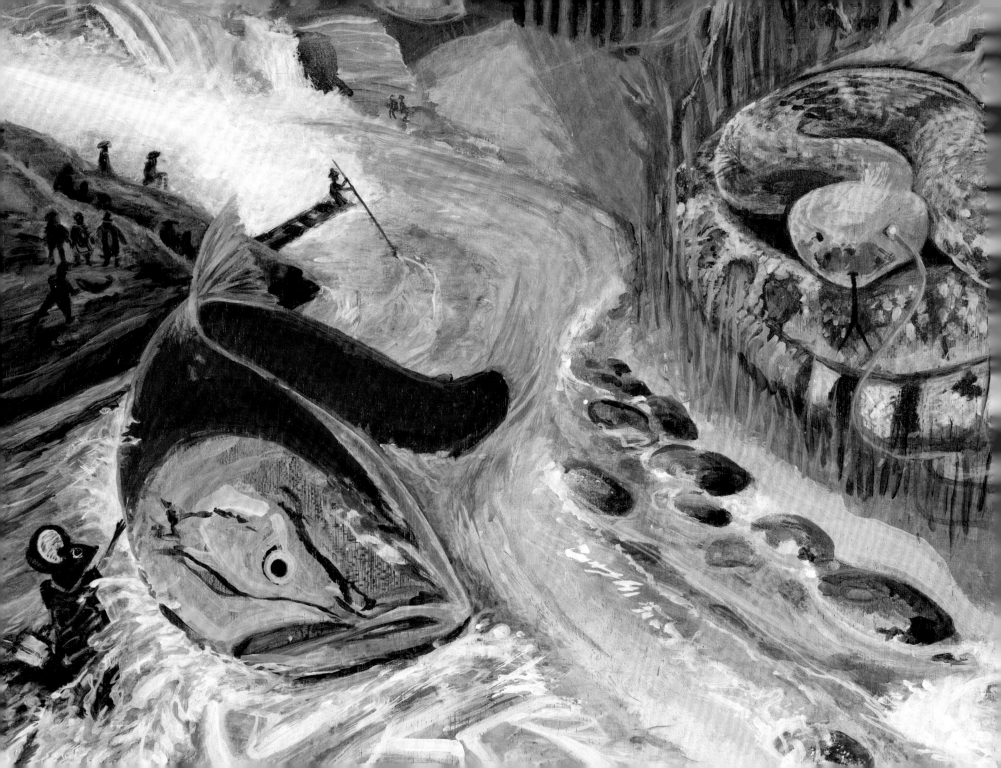

That arrow point bone that's in the skull, it's like a tree - for each year the salmon is in the ocean, it leaves a line in the skull. You can actually boil down the skulls and see how many years they stayed in the ocean before they came back up to spawn. It's three to five years that most salmon spend in the ocean before they come back up to spawn. You can see what the travels of that fish were. It's like a watermark, but it's in the skull, just like a growth ring in a tree, so you can see, there's another year, there's another year, there's another year.

K'tunk, Kettle Falls, is also in the Sturgeon-Nosed Canoe story. It was quite a spot in terms of connecting beings to the landscape. The repetitive nature of certain places is because those places were very important. *K'tunk* being the southern boundary of Sinixt *tum xúlaʔxʷ*, that's where a lot of the base stories are from. *K'tunk* was such an iconic place to Sinixt People in terms of our plenitude, in terms of our status as the keepers of the river. When they talk about the Salmon Chief in Sinixt, that was the main chief of the entire *Snx̌ʷntkʷitkʷ*, the Columbia River system. Until the Sinixt Salmon Chief said it was okay to fish, no one downstream, right down to the mouth of *Snx̌ʷntkʷitkʷ*, was allowed to fish. The Sinixt Salmon Chief would authorize the release of fishing based on the return for the biological purposes of spawning. When we saw the return of the salmon here in the headwaters, then the Salmon Chief could release everyone downriver to fish.

Lewis and Clark's journals talk about how, on *Snx̌ʷntkʷitkʷ* down in Yakima country, fish were so plentiful in the river you could walk across their backs, but the Indians were so lazy that they wouldn't get off their backsides and fish. What they didn't realize is that they didn't have permission to fish yet.

The Salmon Chief system was part of a <u>huge</u> conservation activity, cross-referenced by <u>many</u> tribes who used *Snx̌ʷntkʷitkʷ* for that food source.

It's that whole settler mentality of, oh well, if there's food there you can just go at it, not realizing there were laws and rules around conservation and if you didn't have permission, you'd get spanked. So there are a lot of stories about the salmon like this one where he is the main character and *K'tunk* is the setting, the seat of the Salmon Chief.

Everybody did every kind of fishing at *K'tunk*. It wasn't just one form. Where you might have weirs in one place, there would be catch nets in another, where fish would jump up and be captured on these platforms and people would gather them. Some people used dip nets out on scaffold-like apparatuses and they'd dip their nets down into the falls where the salmon were jumping and catch the salmon as they were going up the falls. Then there was gaffing; it's a kind of spearing. The Slocan River, *Słuqin*, basically means speared through the head. All of those forms of fishing take a lot of skill, a lot of strength; you're basically in a falls where it's misty, it's slippery and you've got a 30-or 40-pound salmon wrestling on the end of a spear or in a dip net. That's a lot to handle, even now, it's a lot to reel in. Everybody had their own special way they liked to do things. That's where all those practices were engaged – it wasn't one technique over another, but certain kinds of fishing techniques were more effective in some places than others.

**Back then, it was like it is today,
you carry on the tradition of
how your family did things,
where the expertise in your family was.**

One of my first memories as a child, when I was barely walking, was being on a creek. The creek was glittering with shimmering orange flecks from the *kíkniʔs*, the kokanee, swimming in the creek. I remember there were three galvanized wash tubs which is how we used to do our laundry back in the day. There were two men and three or four women and a bunch of us kids. The men were actually gaffing these *kíkniʔs* and throwing them up on the grassy edges of the creek. A gaff is a spear with a hook on it, a kind of apparatus that you stab the fish with and pull them out of the water as they're swimming by. In terms of the gaff itself, there's a two-pronged one but also a one-sided one. You have to have a special talent to know, first of all, where to stab the fish, because part of the gaffing requires you to jerk the gills. You're stabbing and jerking back and then throwing the fish out onto the shore.

It was the job of the women to club the fish that were thrown onto the shore and throw them into these galvanized tubs. I was too little to do anything except hang over the edge of the tub and watch the fish flop around, but all those fish flopping and slithering in these wash tubs impressed me. The plenitude that represented to me and the excitement of the communal gathering and the impression of the fish in the stream! And how

adept the men were at hitting those fish and flicking them back onto the shore of the creek. Oh course, the women too were quick – bam! Into the tub! And bam! Into the tub!

**It was such a beautiful,
shimmering mass of movement
as the *kíkniʔs* were going up.
It was just amazing to me.**

I was so young. That is my earliest memory. I'm glad I retained it. It had to be really impressive because I don't have many memories after that until I'm much older.

At completion, the washtubs were loaded into the pickup. All of us kids, back in the day, seven or eight of us squished together in the back seat of the pickup with these three tubs in the box of the pickup and off we went. I don't remember how they were taken care of. That would have been the dull part, the gutting and processing of the fish. They were probably doing a combination of things – smoking, drying, canning, freezing; back then canning was really big. I can remember back in the 50s my Mom and Dad getting a freezer and that being a pretty progressive possession to have. At the time, my grandmother's refrigerator was a little screened-in box off the back of the house.

When Jim Gouk was the Member of Parliament in this area, he was in touch with me when the Okanagans were over here exerting their fishing rights in Sinixt territory. They went out and tried gaffing fish but didn't have the proper equipment nor the strength to pull the fish out. They were basically spearing them and gutting them without killing them properly. The fish were dying without being utilized in any way. It incensed a lot of the sports fisherman in the territory and they came to us, the Sinixt People, not only blaming us but also holding us responsible for how these other Indians were behaving in regards to this resource. It's just like Coyote, "oh yeah, I do that all the time, I gaff fish all the time". But they come in and obviously can't gaff a fish and pull it out of the water. They can stab it and wound it and make it die, but they can't actually complete the task of taking a fish in that manner.

It incensed me, first of all that the Okanagans would come over here and claim fishing rights without asking permission from the Sinixt, which is protocol. That they would come over and exert these rights that they don't have with very poor practices, is sacrilege.

**Damaging fish and killing these fish,
without being able to utilize that meat
is contrary to all our beliefs about
the sacredness of life.**

A SETTLER'S REFLECTION:

I am an unsettled settler as far as my conscience goes, considering the legacy of attempted genocide of the people on whose lands I settle. It has been through listening to the land and stories of Sinixt people such as Bob Campbell, Robert Watt and Ernie Ksaws' Brooks that I have come into relationship with the longer story of displacement and cultural revival that is omitted from the official narratives of Canada. This land is unceded which means it was never surrendered to the Crown. As a Canadian, I feel like a pirate here sitting on stolen booty.

The story of the Rattlesnake and the Salmon made numerous impressions on me. The way it was embedded in the landscape with imagery of the river, the animals and their interactions, I could almost hear the gurgling of *Snx̌ʷntkʷitkʷ*. I felt chills as Salmon was described as being loved for his red, handsome face. I felt soothed by the familiar image of Salmon's sun-bleached body washing up on the sandbar. It was as if the story of Rattlesnake and Salmon itself is constantly and timelessly arising from the landscape. As a scatterling in the settler-colonial diaspora, this satisfies my deep longing for the Spirit of Place.

Another part of its beauty was the weaving of multiple origin stories into its narrative: the rattlesnake's belly-crawl; the arrow point in Salmon's head; how the timber wolves were directed to their lands by Salmon and how Salmon himself is enshrined as cultural hero and Chief.

This story could be a Big Story in mythic terms. The strongest image is Salmon as hero. I've witnessed the strength of Salmon's regenerative capacity in spawning channels and, in this story, his death and resurrection put both Salmon and Mouse into an archetypal Christ-like position for the tenacity of their devotion. The reverence I know Indigenous People have for both the Salmon and the cultural laws of the Salmon Chief could only be paralleled in Western terms by the reverence people have for the saviour and hero archetype.

Coming home to the sacredness of Salmon also feels like a homecoming for me personally as a descendant of displaced Celtic people - Celts recognized the Salmon of Knowledge as existing within a complex cosmology that I am rediscovering. I grieve the ocean-going Salmon when I see their land-locked Kokanee cousins spawn and would rather dismantle dams such as the Grand Coulee than continue to cut them off from this land. May the Salmon one day return!

GABRIEL KECZAN

HOW TURTLE GOT HIS TAIL

Turtle, hoping to win one of the three tails *Spəpelinaʔ,* Rabbit had won, challenged *Spəpelinaʔ* to a race. *Spəpelinaʔ* agreed, confident he would win. On the day of the race, *Spəpelinaʔ* quickly left Turtle behind. At various points along the race trail, he stopped to nap since Turtle was so slow. Every time Turtle passed him, *Spəpelinaʔ* woke up and passed him again. The last time he napped, he slept too long and Turtle passed him and crossed the finish line first. Turtle's winnings were to pick between the three tails offered by *Spəpelinaʔ* – rabbit's tail, bear's tail and frog's tail. He picked the frog's tail because it matched him best and he wears that tail to this day.

Story told by Taress Alexis

Art by Amélie Blanchard

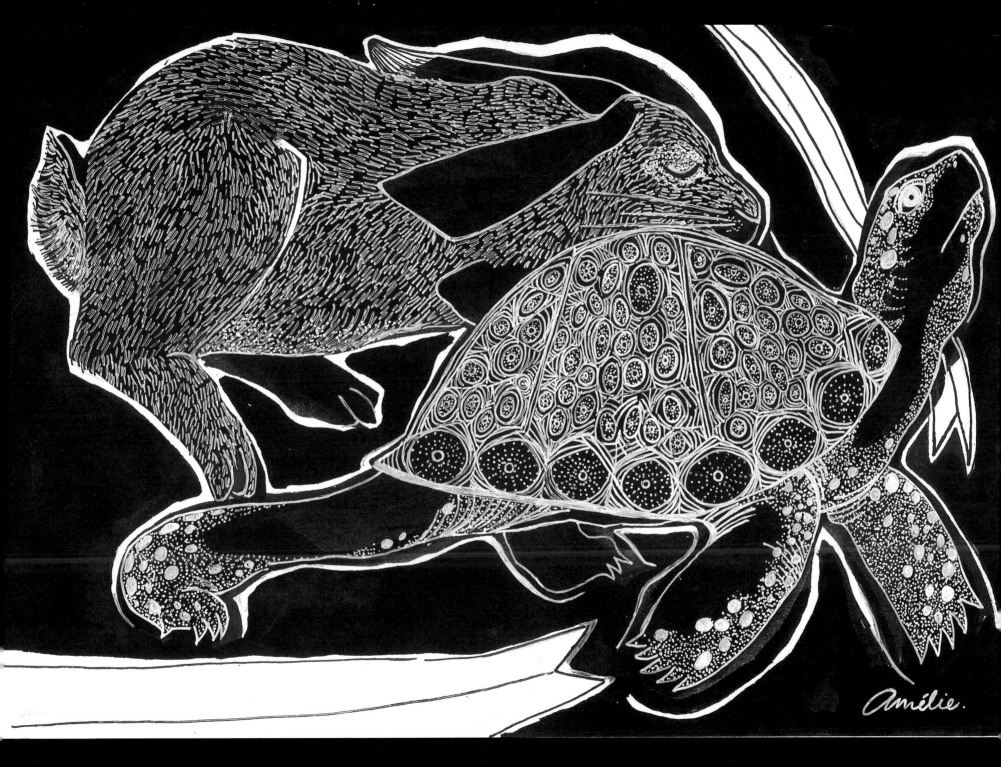

Amélie.

I don't think this story was in the original *Coyote Stories* book by Mourning Dove. This one has probably been borrowed from the European stories, but it's been modified. Like most of the creature feature stories it has an exchange or gift in it. It might have been adopted, in part, to teach about turtles but also to teach about ego and competition.

Sinixt culture has a very different perspective on competition from contemporary culture.

In the last few years, a focus in the local school district has been around wanting to engage children in games the Sinixt might have played. What would those games have been and would there have been someone out there teaching games to children?

In other Indigenous traditional cultures, there are games being played, like lacrosse and the Haudenosaunee snowsnake game, but neither are games children would play. The most engaged form of these games were between communities – who would actually host the snowsnake itself and the dynamics of those exchanges. If you look at games like lacrosse and others, they were very much adult games, they weren't organized for little children.

Having engaged in the process of what it's like being around colonial children, it's always about having to be entertained – plug them into this or plug them into that. There is some aspect of children having to be engaged beyond life into games and competition. Asking around and remembering conversations, I wondered: What is it that we did? And it finally dawned on me that we didn't really have children's games. It doesn't mean that children didn't play or that children didn't have fun, but there weren't any specific games developed for the entertainment of children.

Children engaged in fun by learning life skills.

Boys would be given bows and arrows and slings and basically be told, go kill something. Bring a rabbit home for the soup pot. Chase deer through the woods. Those boys then learned how to dress the meat. They learned these skills as children to develop skills that they would need to produce and survive. Little girls did the same thing – they were given dolls, they were taught how to weave baskets, how to make moccasins, how to cook, how to preserve and store the food. There was a cooperative resonance between the genders. If meat was brought into the village, it belonged to the women, and they would have to take some responsibility for the cutting up, the sharing, the distribution of those goods. Girls needed to learn that too.

In terms of adult games, I spent a lot of my youth – until I was directed not to by a spiritual man – playing stick game, or as they call it in Canada, *ha la hal*. It's a gambling game but it's more a team sport than contemporary gambling. You have a leader and you sing their song. Your village or your team is carrying an aspect of the family. That song is one aspect of life. That song carries luck, that song carries power. People take these songs to the Winter Dance pole and sing them to infuse them again with luck and with power. That's how you care for your song.

If that is not your family song, if you don't have permission to sing it, it is like other cultural belongings, you don't sing it. The songs belong to someone. If you're playing stick game, you might gravitate to those songs that have more power, that are lucky – Oh it sounds really good when people sing it together – and be drawn in to participate in that team.

As people sing those songs, it becomes an act of culture, it becomes an act of commitment to take a side and to support the power of one song over another song.

There'd be great bets and carryings on, but not like the gambling of today. Those stick games might last for hours and hours or even days if those power structures, those songs, were well matched. Those sticks go back and forth. One side might like look like it's losing and you're thinking – oh, no, no, no – and all of sudden those songs pick up power and all those sticks come back to you. Oh! You're infused again! And when the teams are even, it becomes a very settled kind of thing.

Competition is not in respect to colonial ideas of competition. There are points of this competitive structure that are well beyond a person, even well beyond humanity even. They are about a song, they're about acquiring a song, about a family that holds that song, about acquiring that song. It's not about being the competitor or being the winner. Even in the days of those days, like the snowsnake, one village competed against another. Those games can be deadly, you can get roughed up. But it's not about you as an individual even though you might be assessed as a good lacrosse player.

Your skills and your skill sets were about bringing honour and acknowledgment to your place, to your village, to your people, not necessarily to you, even though you might be touted as one of the best.

We have a different idea today about our belongings, be they physical or cultural, and how we take care of them. You'd carry pride, for example, if you had the best horse. That meant you took care of it and it meant the horse held some position in your life that was higher than you. It's not about ownership. That horse's skills are not your skills, that horse's skills are that horse's skills. That pony represents a place you should be proud of.

In colonial times, these sort of competitions have become skewed and skewed in a colonial manner. A good example is the Indian car. If you watch the movie Smoke Signals, there's a car that would only drive in reverse and it had a coat hanger for an antenna. In the olden days it wouldn't matter how beat up your car was, it would have a position in your life. It might be a wreck but you would keep it cleaned and it would have a position in your life, because many people didn't have a car at all. You would show some pride in what that represents and not run it down by not taking care of it. You would take care of it, just like that pony. You would not take the best pony in the village and not feed it, not give it water, or not take care of it.

Competition becomes more of a collective fulfillment than a personal fulfillment of "oh, I'm the best."

Competition in contemporary times becomes more about an egotism, not about a team. In team sports these days, you have people who are recognized in say, football. People say, my paycheque is bigger than your paycheque is. It's not about teams anymore, it becomes about personalities. They turn the people into the pony instead of the team.

A good lacrosse player was still part of the collective – honoured for their skills but not pulled out of the collective and made into an icon and thus creating inequity. Again, people wanted to hold a prideful place. You wanted to make the best basket, you wanted to be a person who could produce and do things in a good way. It wasn't about I'm doing this and I'm the best. Everyone would aspire to be a master not because I'm me-me-me but because of the position you hold in the collective. They look at them as the person who holds the responsibility and that's where the buck stops.

Creating that position wasn't necessarily about creating a position to fulfill your ego but to develop your level of responsibility within that fulfillment. You become the person other people come to generate knowledge – be it spiritual or skill-oriented - collaboratively. If you took those concepts and applied a colonial perspective, you can skew them and make it about ego, you can skew them and make them about power, control and all of those things.

If you look at it from a collective perspective,
a community perspective,
a survival perspective,

then you see all pieces
of the whole community worked together
to create survival.

It isn't about position. It is everything to do with equity. I might be good at this thing but I'm not good at something else. You develop skills around those things that you've demonstrated a sign of skill around. That becomes your position then in that collective, as opposed to that competition. You step up to that plate of that responsibility. It doesn't mean you step up to the plate to be number one.

If you look at the landscape and aspects of landscape in these stories, everything's important. If you look at the little frog in the Frog Mountain story, who shared his love and who wasn't a big piece of meat, it wasn't about being the most powerful being in this *tum xúlaʔxʷ*. It was about every aspect of this existence having a place, which represents their place of power within the collective. Within that collective it's all equal, not about who's a bigger piece of meat, who's a bigger threat, etc.

It's about everyone stepping up
to the plate and contributing what they can.
You develop your skills as much as you develop them.
There is no expectation that you will be the greatest.

Who remembers the moments in their youth when they decided they were going to be someone or do something great in their lifetime? I do. I wanted to be the next Margaret Atwood. Famous.

Who remembers making deals with themselves? If I'm not a famous _____ by the time I'm 30, I'll do something else. I do. I forget how many published books I'd set my sights on or what kind of acclaim I'd hoped for, but it certainly hadn't happened. And I was doing what I loved, I was fully engaged in my life. Still, I'd look at other people's successes and wonder why the Globe and Mail wasn't reviewing my books, why the big publishers weren't knocking at my door.

My culture was telling me that either you're a star, or you're no one; pack up and go home. And I looked at the Star Writers, the people who were getting the reviews and the acclaim. I could see that they weren't necessarily better (or worse) writers than I was but they were willing to play the game, do the schmoozing, put the leg work into the competition of Being Known. I liked my life the way it was and I didn't have the ego required to get out there and push. In my mid-30s, when my first novel came out, I tried. I didn't like it. It wasn't my way. I tried giving up writing but I couldn't. This is my gift and I owe it my attention regardless of how many people read what I write.

**It's about everyone stepping up to the plate
and contributing what they can.
You develop your skills as much as you develop them.**

There is no expectation that you will be the greatest.

So, now at 55, I'm not a famous writer and certainly no Margaret Atwood. But I'm happy with my accomplishments. I've developed my skills. I'm as proud of my books as I am of my ability to write a good press release, as I am of being the editor and publisher of this book. It's possible that this book will be the one I'm most proud of bringing into the world. It's a relief that I got here. I would have been much happier in my youth if my expectations, my family's expectations and my culture's expectations had been about contributing, about being me, instead of running the rat race.

KL KIVI

CHRISTINA LAKE

There was a split among the Sinixt over how they wanted to be and some people decided to migrate. The people who left were tied to a more spiritual way of being. They travelled for many years and arrived in the valley where Christina Lake is now. There was only water there during the freshet in spring and the rest of the year the valley was dry. Still the people wanted to stay there and began to pray. They prayed the water up and up it came until it became a huge lake which was known to the Sinixt People as *ncaʔlíwm*. The people who lived there became known as the *incaʔlíwm*, which means the people of *ncaʔlíwm*. The river that flows out of that lake, flows down to the modern day community of Inchelium on the Colville Reservation in the USA, where many Sinixt live.

Story told by Marilyn James

Art by Amber Santos

The people from Christina Lake wanted to know the story of how it came to be. The contemporary story of how Christina Lake got its name is from a woman named Christina McDonald or McDougal who was the daughter of a chief from that area. She was well known and well liked, and that's how Christina Lake got its name. Some people from Grand Forks and Christina Lake asked me to tell the story but I didn't know it.

Eva Orr and my mom, Alvina Lum, were still alive, and so I sat down with them and said we have a request for this story: do you remember? And they both sat there, kind of like how we've been discussing stories, and couldn't exactly remember just how the story went.

**That's how mom and Eva were,
remembering bits of the story,
neither one of them remembering
the entire story by themselves.**

But Eva began, and where her memory lapsed, my mom's memory picked up the thread of the story, and when my mom's thread ran out, Eva picked it up, and so on. Between those two old ladies, the story of Christina Lake came to light. I'm not sure this story was ever documented, or if it was just part of the oral history that both my mom and Eva knew. I'd never seen it in print or heard it before. I'd heard that the name came from Christina McDougal or McDonald, but I'd never heard the actual story of how the lake itself came to be.

The people separated into a migration group that left the main group at the Columbia Mountains up by Revelstoke, way north. This group broke off and ended up in what is now known as Christina Lake, but there was no water there to begin with. The people wanted to stay there as they had traversed almost the entire length of our *tum xúla?xʷ*, being at the southern end. When they prayed up the water there, the Sinixt People's name for that place was *nca?líwm*. And the people who, in the story, brought the water up out of the ground that became Christina Lake, were called *inca?líwm*.

**In that historical movement of Sinixt People
across the landscape they became
the inchelium people from *nca?líwm*,
Christina Lake.**

They were pushed out of Canada onto a place now called Inchelium on the Colville Reservation, and it's mostly Sinixt People there. Those Sinixt are thinking it's a place name when it's really the name of a group of people who came from *nca?líwm*.

The migration and movement of Sinixt People have occurred across the landscape. At many times it is only these stories that pull the people back to their existence on the landscape historically. What happened at Midway and *kpiƛls* are two other examples.

As the Sinixt People were being forced across the border by the military at the Midway area, they twisted two saplings together and that's called the Entwined Tree. It was a prayer by the Sinixt People being forced down across the border that the People would never, ever forget their tie to this land; that there would always be that connection. Those trees still stand and are part of the landscape, down by the clinic in Midway.

**The people being forced out wanted a symbol,
an understanding of themselves as a People
and a connection to the landscape.**

If you come east you end up in Castlegar, where Alex Christian's family lived at *kpiƛls*, which is now known as Brilliant, across the river from Castlegar. *kpiƛls* is an area that represents a huge contemporary issue. It represents the tremendous need to dialogue about our settler-Sinixt or settler-Indian relationships. What has created the foundation for those relationships has been some pretty bad behaviour.

One of the last Sinixt People living in the area was Alex Christian at *kpiƛls*. Right there at *kpiƛls* was a huge Sinixt burial ground and Alex Christian was the caretaker. Some of those were contemporary graves, square ones, not just the ancient round ones. The Indian Agent of the day (early 1900s) mistakenly and erroneously sold that land to the Doukhobors. Alex Christian wrote many letters and begged and begged to have that land set aside for a reserve. The Doukhobors plowed to the door of Alex Christian's home and staked the skulls of Alex Christian's ancestors around his family home. They built a fence so high and tight around Alex Christian's home that the only access they had to their house was via the Columbia River. Alex Christian's sister Mary-Anne was murdered and left on the tracks by the jam factory there. No one was ever charged. He feared for the

life of his daughter and moved his family down to a cabin just below the US-Canadian border on the Columbia River. He still traveled up the Columbia by canoe though to access his trap lines at Genelle, Blueberry, *kpiƛls*, and Kootenay Lake.

**Those are the behaviours that created
a real barrier to communication
between Sinixt and settler cultures.**

And of course, with the declared extinction the government created a black hole in terms of information about the Sinixt, making fertile ground for settler minds to conjure up stories to say there weren't any Indians here. These stories absented us from this landscape, when we know that many of our People who lived here in seasonal rounds would have had homes in several areas. They would have four or five homes around their little area where they'd hunt and fish and then move on to their next house area. There were many incidents where settlers gunned down Sinixt People for trying to come back and reclaim their home places.

The violence we experienced was a designed response to Indian People because the government had known all along it wanted this region. Within the settler culture, it needed to create a certain mentality about how to deal with those Indian People. *They need to be controlled. They're just wandering the ground like wild things.*

**What the government should really look at
is how to preserve what we have**

- Peoples and lands -
and make them jewels instead of
driving people off and paving paradise.

Putting a parking lot in an alpine area and calling that a vacation is part of that mentality. There are these approaches of how we look at landscape, what is acceptable, and what isn't acceptable. Once you hit one of those mental barriers and you're talking about cultural practices, it becomes very easy for Sinixt People to be dismissed completely out of the equation because we've always stood for our autonomy. We've stood behind our laws to protect this water, this land. Many of the other Indians who are recognized and are claiming our land are highly colonized, ready to sign on the dotted line for a dollar. A lot of horrendous things happen in the name of that political game, and for political recognition.

A SETTLER'S REFLECTION:

As a settler scholar who studies Western Canadian literature, I spend a lot of time unpacking the stories settlers tell ourselves about our place on stolen Indigenous territories. More often than not, those stories involve a wilful forgetting, or not knowing. Not knowing the stories of the land and its People is something we settlers are particularly adept at. It's a skill we've honed to legitimize our thefts. Reading and listening to Marilyn James' words, and particularly this story, again makes me acutely aware of the gaps in my knowledge. While the colonial violence of displacement, particularly in this story, has meant that "people don't associate *incaʔlíwm*, which means the people of *ncaʔlíwm* with the people from Inchelium…, not knowing that story," I feel deeply how much the colonial project has cost the Sinixt People, and what it has and will cost settlers who continue to live as strangers to the land and its stories.

I am powerfully struck by the symbol of the Entwined Tree in this story. The Entwined Tree serves as a memorial to the forced exile of the Sinixt People from their territory across the border (a particularly violent manifestation of colonial dominance) and as "a symbol, an understanding of themselves as a People and a connection to the landscape." In his 1993 one-man show, *Fronteras Americanas*, Guillermo Verdecchia, who was born in Argentina and exiled to Canada as a young man, struggles with the concept of home and belonging. At one point in the play, Verdecchia's protagonist is diagnosed by an Argentinian medicine man as having "a very bad border wound," and told that he must come to terms with the fact this wound, the border,

"is . . . home." The act of entwining of saplings in James' story, feels like a powerful way of acknowledging and moving to heal a border wound.

In many ways, I feel like many of us are living with border wounds; living with the ongoing and painful consequences of the violent and appropriative colonial project. Settlers, heirs and beneficiaries of the project (I include myself here), benefit greatly from forgetting, but forgetting is untenable and it is immoral: we need to acknowledge and move to heal the wounds our ancestors and we have inflicted on Indigenous Peoples, on the land, and on ourselves.

What settler would not want to forget what happened to Alex Christian, his sister and the bones of his ancestors? But what is our moral footing as settlers if we choose to forget, or do not know, that settlers unearthed Sinixt graves and staked the skulls of Christian's ancestors around his family home as intimidation. We need to know these stories, to know the deep history of the place we've called home, and to know what our responsibilities are. Knowing these stories, I believe, will change our present and future relationships with Indigenous communities and with the land on which we dwell. This is difficult work, but it's our work to do.

RENÉE JACKSON-HARPER

IN THE SHADOW OF EXTINCTION

The Adolph family decided to go gold panning near Revelstoke in order to survive the winter on the Colville Reservation. Ambrose Adolph was the designated driver of their Model T Ford. They ended up in a huge cottonwood grove where Ambrose went to hunt grouse. There, up in the crotches of the cottonwoods, he was amazed to see stacks of caribou antlers up to three feet tall. It was an ancient Sinixt hunting place where migrating caribou were hunted. The hunters sat in the nests of antlers that they removed from the ground to keep the way clear for the caribou. Ambrose always kept that place in his mind. When he was away at war (WWII), he would think of this place, and think that if he survived he would go back there. When he returned, all that was left were fences and fields.

Story told by Marilyn James as learned from Bob Campbell and Ambrose Adolph

Art by Tyler Toews

This was a story I heard many, many years ago and always wanted a chance to hear it from the actual teller themself. I finally heard it from Bob Campbell; the original story was from his uncle Ambrose who lived down on the Colville Reservation. For the Adolph family, the original landscape for their family was the area around Revelstoke, which is the northern part of Sinixt *tum xúlaʔxʷ*. The Columbia Mountains above Revelstoke are where Sinixt territory sprouts and are where this story takes place. As you know, 80% of our territory was in Canada and 20% in the USA.

In the early days, the Colville Reservation in the USA, which is a confederation of 12 different tribes, used to come all the way to the Canadian border. Because that northern half was all Sinixt territory and because we're a very seasonal-round, gathering kind of People, we constantly traversed the US-Canadian border. Eventually what was considered the north half of the reservation was diminished by executive order – just stroked away by a US government pen. It removed the Sinixt who were on the Rez far enough away so that they wouldn't be constantly crossing that US-Canada border. It further impoverished all of the Sinixt People who were forced out of Canada and went and lived on the Colville Reservation. There was no economic base on the Rez even though they were growing some vegetables and doing some farming. Their main mode of sustenance had always been and was still hunting and gathering.

At the Colville Rez
you couldn't hunt enough
you couldn't gather enough.

Condensed population
condensed space
to hunt,
to gather,
to survive.

A lot of the root fields were beyond the Reservation borders and so it really restricted the Indian People's existence. This story is at the time when people were suffering because there wasn't enough to eat and there weren't any jobs. What Ambrose Adolph was really adamant about in my visits with him, was that his family was lucky because they had an alternative way to survive. The majority had no alternatives – he said over and over again, what a pitiful time it was for Indians on the Rez.

**When it comes to survival
and the survival of your People,
that's the time you use everything
in your power to create that for your families.**

The majority had no alternatives – there was no welfare, there were no food stamps, there were no resources except themselves for survival. He talked about how rough it was and when they would go out and maybe get a deer and others would come and ask for meat. They had no way to get out to hunt, a lot of them didn't have guns – that was an expense - they didn't have bullets, they didn't have gas, rigs, nothing. They lived in a trepidatious state of existence. He reiterated over and over again how hard it was when they were cordoned onto the Rez. Even this trip had to be done in a clandestine way.

It was hard being cordoned onto the Rez
They weren't allowed in Canada.
They snuck across the border.
It was hard being cordoned onto the Rez

Like Ambrose, my Dad had an interesting story to tell me about a large herd of caribou that used to migrate down through the Selkirks and Purcells to a place almost due south of here, called Moses Lake, in Washington. He couldn't understand why the caribou would migrate all the way down to Moses Lake, swim in that lake and then return north. There's less than 30 tribal members in that Selkirk caribou herd now. Of these thousands and thousands of animals that's all that's left today. They don't migrate down to Moses Lake anymore.

The first big wipeout of the caribou
was due to the gold rush.

The miners came here and had meat smoking and processing places along the Arrow Lakes. The settlers would go and kill the caribou by the hundreds, like they did the buffalo on the prairies. They would take the two back hindquarters and smoke them and then send the meat to the gold fields in Alaska and in Northern BC. Apparently, caribou by the thousands were killed during this gold rush area.

As settlers began settling the area, like Ambrose said, open spaces were dissected by fences and fields. It becomes critical for the survival of migratory animals for settlers and people to make way for those travel corridors, but that was never considered.

Fences tend to stop the migratory patterns
and pathways of migrating animals.

Habitat is critical for these kinds of animals and when there's no old growth for them to eat, or they're thwarted from moving around, it diminishes their capacity for survival. The caribou cows are pregnant through most of the winter but give birth in late winter, early spring. They really need access in that calving season to the lichens that grow on old-growth trees in this region. Up north, they go to the land lichens on the frozen tundra. Because the Ministry of Forest has chosen to harvest all of the old growth areas, access to old-growth lichens in this region is practically non-existent.

Caribou cows need that lichen
in order to lactate.

Of course, highways claim caribou, even with these low numbers we have. There have been caribou hit by cars in the Salmo-Creston Pass on Highway 3. Up in the mountains, caribou are being terrorized by snowmobiles as well. The snowmobile tracks make it possible for the predators to get to them whereas in the past the predators would have been stopped by the deep snow.

I've tried to address some of the issues around the trans-location of animals in the past and had a hard time doing that. The Ministry and their techniques for trans-location of caribou are not acceptable. They would go in the late fall, early winter when there's snow on the ground and they'd chase them with helicopters to gun-net pregnant females. Sometimes they'd be slammed to the ground and sometimes there wasn't enough snow for the animals not to be slammed onto rocks.

And if they're run by the helicopters long enough,
the females that are pregnant will slip their calves.
If they're slammed to the ground
hard enough they'll slip their calves.
They'll slip their calves.

And if they're slammed to the ground hard, it may bruise the entire side of a caribou body and because mass tissue bruising causes an issue called necropathy, which occurs when there's not enough circulation through the system, they'll just begin rotting alive and die.

We tried to address some of these issues on a tribal to tribal basis. The tribal People up in the Chilcotin area, where these animals were coming from, could have hunted them from horseback. They could have net-fenced certain areas down valleys and driven them into those areas and brought them in in a gentle way. Instead, the Ministry penned the traumatized caribou up and waited until they could gun-net enough of them. Then their antlers were sawed off. Then, they're brought to a very strange area where they've never been before. They're turned loose in an area and they have no way of defending themselves because they have no antlers.

Ministry biologists were taking the pregnant females, corralling them up in the Salmo-Creston pass and feeding them alfalfa. Even though it was Grade A alfalfa they were feeding them, the caribou could literally bust a gut eating it because they can't get any nutrition from it. They were starving these pregnant females because all they were giving them was alfalfa. And when they turn them loose with their calves, because they have to, there's no old-growth trees for these females to get the lichens they need for their babies' survival.

You can see how this species
is being managed to extinction.

When you have just a few who are trying to struggle on the land, it begins to be pretty painful to watch and relate to when you're someone whose responsibility it is to take care of them. And of course, none of our Indian People's suggestions of ways to enhance these different caribou herds are ever paid attention to. None of them. The Ministry just has contractors with helicopters and biologists who don't know anything about how to take care of caribou.

I don't have any faith in that system
whatsoever
to address this situation.

Even trying to go to the Ministry of Forests and asking "what's on the chopping block?" Asking, why, especially in the Salmo-Creston region, every old-growth area is targeted for cutting, every single one? Can't the Ministry of Forests talk to the Ministry of Environment and tell them that caribou need lichen and old-growth forest to survive? Of course the Ministries know that but they won't pull out their big stick and whip the Ministry of Forests. Of course, if they chose to exercise species at risk laws, if they chose to have a serious commitment to their management strategies and really were committed to managing caribou for anything other than extinction, they could. I've always said, it is not management of caribou, it is not management of predators, it is not management of forests, it is management of people that needs to exist.

Let's get rid of all these Ministries and have a Ministry of Human Behaviour.

A good example of their bad management choices is the killing off of wolves and other predators. If the government can't actually take care of the few animals that are here, killing off other animals is not going to fix it. It's not the predators that are the problem. The problem is the caribou don't have the habitat they need. But they'll kill every wolf because they have to put the blame somewhere and it always ends up that way. Predators are just predators, they're just who they are. If caribou weren't hunted and slaughtered out of existence by settler culture, we'd still have healthy populations of caribou. Up in the Chilcotin, they're still a sustainable meat source for the Indian People. They're not what they used to be but they're still huntable and a feature of the territory.

Where here, the caribou are like the Sinixt,

they're just a shadow of the landscape.
You don't see them, and when you do see them it's kind of a vision because they're so rare. And it was such a natural aspect to this landscape in the past. Right now, I'd really rather not have caribou than see them suffer.

147

A SETTLER'S REFLECTION:

The story of the mountain caribou and how it parallels the experiences of the Sinixt feels particularly poignant. Both have had their seasonal-round way of life obliterated by colonial settlement and our fences. Both have been driven off the land that ensured their survival for millennia up until the current colonial era. Both the Sinixt and the caribou are now few in number, a scattered diaspora in places where they have had to eke out a bare existence. Both have been subjected to violence, dispossession and outright slaughter, be it by introduced diseases or for the purposes of food.

When I think of Ambrose Adolph returning from war to look for that place that held such a potent aura of his People's long relationship with the caribou, I feel immeasurably sad. What if I went away to fight for some stranger's land and came home to find that same stranger had taken my own? When this kind of displacement happens in other places in the world, we call the people it happens to refugees.

Today's Sinixt <u>are</u> the descendants of refugees.
They were the refugees of the West Kootenay.
They were chased out to make room for settlers,
for <u>us</u>.

Like other refugees, the Sinixt fled their homeland because of oppression, dispossession and violence, just like Syrians, just like Eritreans, Guatemalans, Palestinians, Tibetans, etc. of today. Why would we think of the Sinixt any differently than all the refugees our communities and country are currently reaching out to help? According to the United Nations, "a refugee... is a displaced person who has been forced to cross national boundaries and who cannot return home safely." Displacement is a long-lasting reality for most refugees and yet refugee status, under international law, cannot be inherited unless you are Palestinian. At the same time, the UN's Pinheiro Principles are "guided by the idea that people not only have the right to return home, but also the right to the same property. It seeks to return to the pre-conflict status quo and ensure that no one profits from violence."

How do I benefit from the historic and current dispossession of the Sinixt? This question initiates a giant pause for me. And more thoughts than this page can hold.

I've heard many people echo Marilyn's sentiments about the caribou in speaking about the Sinixt: you don't see them, and when you do see them it's kind of a vision because they're so rare. I would love to see caribou repopulate this land. I would love to see many Sinixt reinhabit their homeland. What would it take? Our readiness to grapple with the great tragedy of the Sinixt and to let our colonial Canadian government know that they cannot manage them out of existence in their *tum xúlaʔxʷ* alongside the mountain caribou?

KL KIVI

REPATRIATION OF REMAINS

In the late 1980s, the Sinixt People returned to their *tum xúlaʔxʷ* in BC when remains of their ancestors were dug out of the gravesites at Vallican during road building. When these ancestral remains were taken to the Royal British Columbia Museum (RBCM) in Victoria, Marilyn James began the extensive negotiations of the repatriation process. The first six remains were returned by the RBCM to the Sinixt on November 25, 1990. They were reburied shortly after in a simple but moving ceremony in Vallican, in the Slocan Valley. The Sinixt were the first Indian People in Canada to repatriate and rebury ancestral remains. To date, Marilyn James has participated in the repatriation and reburial of 64 ancestral remains of her People.

Story told by Marilyn James

Art by Catherine Fisher

The return of our ancestors remains began a long story of following the cultural law of repatriation as an apology to the ancestors. Because when you have to deal with something culturally and ceremonially that you've never dealt with before, you're evolving. You're meeting a need. We never would have dug up our ancestors in the past. We would never have dug up anybody's People. It would have never been necessary for us to have a reburial or repatriation of any kind. It is a profound thing to make it about an apology. Eva Orr, our *smum iem* elder, was very adamant that we follow the cultural law.

Eva Orr was our *smum iem*, our matriarch, our wise, eldest woman.

Smum iem is stepping forward and taking care of what needs to be taken care of. Not many women feel comfortable stepping into that role. Eva was our *smum iem*. I had known about these remains for a long period of time but I was doing other activist work. It was Eva who kept calling me, wanting me to be involved. She eventually sent me a directive – it wasn't an ask – basically telling me I needed to come help get these remains back.

I'm still here, still doing that work.

I was telling the story about the mist coming down during the reburial to Lori Barkley, who is an anthropologist. And I said to her, "how did I know it was a vision as opposed to something I was thinking up in my mind?" "How?" she asked. My point of reference was Dances with Wolves, my point of reference was Hollywood Indians. I had no point of reference for how plainly the beings in the mist were dressed, how they looked. They were these super ancient beings that looked so different from anything I'd experienced from Hollywood or dreamed up in my mind or romanticized about what Indians looked like back into the day. I just knew I'd been given a super gift, to see that we were being greeted by our People from the ancient times. That's when I knew that we'd not only helped the ancestors who were returning but we'd helped the village those ancestors came from.

Eva was very adamant that we follow the cultural law and we assist the ancestors to follow the cultural law because they can't do it for themselves. So when we are alive and we know about these laws, we have to assist our ancestors to follow them so they can continue on their journey in the spirit world and the spirit life, and not be stopped from doing that.

We needed to help the ancestors follow the cultural laws because they can't do it for themselves.

We began with those six ancestors on USA Thanksgiving, 1990, and to present we have repatriated 64 remains mostly at the Vallican site. We have replaced some remains where they were dug up or disturbed. That began the journey of repatriation and reburial for the Sinixt People and in 1990 we were the first Indian People to repatriate human remains in Canada. They were doing it in the USA but they hadn't given back any remains here in Canada until we set the precedent. To date, other groups are getting not just human remains but other important cultural articles back from museums and collections.

I'm still here, still doing that work.

Where did other remains come from? Selkirk College, Nakusp Historical Society. There was one set of remains returned from someone's garage attic in Nelson. When Austin Greengrass' house and the whole landscape slipped down three feet, there were remains kicked out of the Earth that we had to gather back up. Archaeologists had to be involved. Austin wanted them there and so we reburied those ancestors there by the Slocan River. Other people, who have chosen to remain anonymous because they have official positions, have given back remains via third parties that they felt they couldn't return to us personally. So a third party intervened to say to us, "come and pick up this box, it's a very important box."

**The remains would speak to Eva
and tell her where they wanted to be.**

When remains came up from the drawdown of *Snx̌ʷntkʷitkʷ*, the Chief of Police in Castlegar called me up and said, "These remains have disinterred from the drawdown of the Columbia and we know they're ancient. We've put them in a box. They're in the janitor's closet. We would like not to have to go through this big rigmarole with different tribal groups coming and fighting over them. We know you've been doing this work, could you just come and get them right away. They're in the janitor's closet."

Basically, in clandestine ways, people are wanting to do the right thing but are wary of the different factions. The politics of who's involved and how they're involved and who should and should not be doing this work can be overwhelming. However, it's so obvious that if we were the first people to repatriate human remains here, we're probably the people to continue doing that work.

I'm still here, still doing that work.

If you find remains, don't handle them. It's not good to be handling human remains because they might take offense, first of all. The second thing is to call and have somebody come and take them away or just replace them somewhere on the property where they won't be disturbed. We've done that before. The legal, colonial protocol is that you call the cops. The cops and the coroner are brought in so they can tell if it's a fresh kill. A coroner can tell right away if they're ancient or whether they should be part of a murder investigation. Then they'll call an archaeologist who will come in and pick the bones up and report about where the bones should go.

We got a set of remains back from Zuckerberg Island by Castlegar. We got some back from *kpix̌ls*, Brilliant, where the Doukhobor Cultural Centre is. There were human remains dug up there that were returned by Mark Mealing from Selkirk College. There was a biology prof at Selkirk College who had a Sinixt skeletal remain on his shelf in the biology lab for many years. He waited until he was retiring, before he felt he could take those remains off the shelf and give them back. For some reason he felt his job would have been jeopardized or there would have been some conflict or controversy around returning them.

**He took those remains off the shelf
and finally gave them back to us.**

People don't understand they can get hurt by those remains if they hang around them. So we do that work, not only for the ancestors but also for the living. We deal with them so that no one gets hurt.

Do I think there are still more remains out there in holdings? The Smithsonian, yes. And in Tribal Collections where they don't know how to deal with them. There might be more remains in museums too, but they often lie. And even if BC Hydro or some other institution has a protocol to consult the Sinixt, the end result is that it still doesn't stop them from disturbing our burials sites if they know they are there. So they may think of themselves as respectful to those remains but the only way to be respectful is to *not* disturb them.

I'm still here, still doing that work.

A SETTLER'S REFLECTION:

This story evokes my ongoing, vengeful desire to go to a local cemetery and dig up some graves. You know, take out the bones and put them in a box and deliver them to a museum or a college or an archaeologist. This fantasy of mine originates from the time I first heard about Sinixt and other Indigenous ancestral remains being unearthed. It comes from the issue Marilyn brings up in this piece:

what, if anything,
will make people understand that disturbing graves
is profoundly disrespectful?

Maybe if I did the same to them, they would understand? However, I know this isn't how people learn respect. Still, I wonder what will make people who have deep respect for their own ancestors, for their own dead, for their own cemeteries, extend that respect to other People's dead ancestors?

So why don't settlers and colonial institutions extend that same respect to the original inhabitants of the places where they've settled? Is it because they lack respect for the Sinixt, for example, and thus it has become okay? Or is it because settlers feel guilty on some level for having displaced Indigenous People and thus, to remove their remains to remove the signs of their long inhabitation on the land settlers claim for themselves? Or is it more insidious than that? Is it a somewhat deliberate attempt by colonial governments and societies to further dishearten and further displace Indigenous People? To attack their ancestral roots so as to oppress as profoundly as possible?

What if I found out that the graves of my grandparents had been dug up and their bones taken away? This is something I've never worried about; it feels so preposterously unlikely. The cemeteries in Estonia where my paternal ancestors are buried, are sacred and revered places. We too are a People who deeply honour our ancestors and visit and tend our burial grounds assiduously. The Brookside Cemetery in Winnipeg, where my maternal grandparents are buried, is also a place towards which people demonstrate respect. If any of their remains were removed, where would my family go to clean graves, light candles, take flowers and commune with our loved ones, with our history?

But what of it? What if I got a call tomorrow saying - your grandparents' bones have been dug up for the expansion of the Winnipeg airport. How would I feel? What would I do? And what if it happened often, as it has for the Sinixt? That it became commonplace any time a burial site of my ancestors was encountered in the path of construction, the bones were dug up and shipped off to a museum or archive? I struggle to even picture it; my settler sense of entitlement is intact on this front. We would never stand for it! To treat my ancestors that way is unthinkably, horrifically wrong. I would feel rage...

KL KIVI

HOW THE *STX̌ÀɬQ* CAME TO KETTLE FALLS

Eagle lived at *K'tunk*, Kettle Falls, with her grandmother. Old *Sxʷƛ́iʔ*, Mountain Goat, lived far up in the mountains. He had sent his eldest son to seek Eagle's hand in marriage. Grandmother Eagle thought her beautiful granddaughter should marry someone better than the eldest *Sxʷƛ́iʔ*, and so organized a race. Old *Sxʷƛ́iʔ* sent his two younger sons to *K'tunk* with a basket of *stx̌àɬq*, huckleberries, and a *Stx̌àɬq* bush to plant, to restore their honour. The eagles decided to let the *sxʷƛ́iʔs* run in the race, although they did not think they stood a chance at winning. As they came to the cliff, the goats raced straight across it, which none of the other animals could do. Grandmother Eagle accepted the gift of *stx̌àɬq*, and Eagle followed the goats back to their home in the mountains. She married the eldest *sxʷƛ́iʔ* and continues to make her nest in the mountains to this day.

Story told by Taress Alexis

Art by Sergio Santos

Story is a way to inform us of what really had a right and a responsibility to be on this landscape that we have impacted. This story goes from simplistic to ultimate. It is a very condensed version. As you mature and grow emotionally and can broaden your perspective, then you get more out of the story. It brings up our law: you give, you bring your best and that's what's expected of you. If you are Sinixt, then according to our laws, you have to look at who is where in the landscape. Who gets to be at the top of the mountains and in the alpine, who is participating on those landscapes, informs us culturally in terms of how we look at the land and our relationships to land. It's bigger than people, it's the environment, and it's how things come.

It's relationship to land.

Everything has its place on the landscape. The goats and the women they married went up to the mountain tops with them, and that's where they are. That's where their environment is, where you will find those specific creatures. Those critters can be on the landscape without causing those particular areas damage, whereas if other critters were to go there and inhabit that area it would change the landscape. Those high alpine areas are very sensitive. If there was, for instance, a migration of caribou through a high alpine area it would mash that alpine and it wouldn't be the same as when only those critters who are meant to inhabit it are there.

What is on the land and where it is on the land informs how you behave on that land. Not the other way around.

You don't go and behave any way you want to. Landscape creates the caveats for your behaviour. It's about knowing how your land is being utilized, by whom, and in what ways you need to approach those landscapes. It doesn't mean you can't go to certain places, but you do it with a level of sensitivity. In our hunting and gathering rounds, if I was there last year, I'm not there the next year or the year after that. I'm there in maybe four or five years.

In that way, conservation takes place. You can say no to yourself.

You can say: I've hunted that area. I'm going to let it come back. I've dug roots from that area. I know it will come back. I know huckleberries are biennial. I'm not going to go back to the same patch every year, I'm going to find the bumper crop this year. I know if I go there next year there won't be the bumper crop because it's biennial. That means you have a very heavy crop, a year off, then you have another bumper crop. You're going to find that other spot on your landscape where there is a bumper crop when it's your biennial spot's year off. You aren't going to go back to the same patch year after year after year, but it doesn't mean you can't ever go back there. Your expectation of what the land is providing you is tempered by what you know the landscape gave you the year before, or what it will give you the next year. You can go to an area and see all the berry bushes with hardly any berries. A great idea is to come back next year!

It's about creating that knowledge of landscape, about knowing the environment.

It's really landscape that informs protocol. Following protocols means even if you are despised, like Grandmother Eagle despised brother *sxʷⱡiʔ*, you still bring a gift. You're always wanting to give your best whether it's accepted or not. And that's the *whuplak'n*, that's the big law, the law of the land. The land tells you what the laws are, the land creates the laws which you observe in order to be in good standing. How did Sinixt People know? How could we be gentle? Because we understood we were part of a community, a living organism. It wasn't about us conquering the environment. It was about us being a functioning aspect within the environment. We got everything we could possibly ever need from that environment, in spades, without having to destroy it. The environment is willing to give itself to you, for you to take, and we understood that. We knew that. We took when we were supposed to take, didn't take when we weren't supposed to take, but we still experienced plenitude because we knew how to be in relationship to the land.

Landscape informs protocol.
***whuplak'n* is the law of the land;**
relationship to land.
The land tells you what the laws are.

A SETTLER'S REFLECTION:

Everything has its place. Everything is a part of the whole. Even if you are despised you still bring a gift. You're obligated to bring your best, whether it is accepted or not. You CAN say no to yourself, you don't just behave any way you want to. As you mature you broaden your perspective and get more and more from these stories.

I like the idea of a society that sets limits, that says: "Hey people, you need to be self-regulating; you need to take responsibility for yourself, others have their own responsibilities, other things they need to take care of. You need to be self-aware, self-motivating." The society I'm living in isn't like that, and I am far from being like that.

I like the idea that you're obligated to give, to bring your best, even if there is no reward. Even if you are not understood, not accepted, or despised. You need to know what you need to do and do it, regardless of how that is accepted. You need to be self-motivating. You need to be self-aware.

I like the idea that everything has its place. That deer shouldn't be up in the high alpine but mountain goat should. You need to know where you should be in the landscape. You need to be self-aware. "But how?" asks 20-year-old me, 30-year-old me, 40-year-old me. As you mature you broaden your perspective and get more and more out of these stories. Keep listening.

CATHERINE FISHER

GLOSSARY OF SINIXT WORDS AND PHRASES

Sinixt spelling – definition (very approximate anglicized prononciation)

ʕayckst – bull trout, after which Sinixt were named (ay-kst)

captikʷɬ - the creation stories of the Sinixt (chaptick-will)

ćṁtus – sturgeon (ts'ntus)

ćskʕáknaʔ - chickadee (zt-skaka-na)

cwix – creek (sweek)

cx̌ʷlúsaʔ – camas (chukaloosa)

kíkniʔ – kokanee, an inland salmonid fish (ki-kee-ni)

kpiƛls – people have bitterroot, Sinixt name for Brilliant BC (ka-pit-ls)

k'tunk- Kettle Falls (k-toonk)

kw'sixw- goose (kwisui)

lim limpt – thank you (lim limpt)

ṁpaʔpaʔsílx – ritually observed year of grieving after the death of a close family member (im-pop-a-seel)

ncaʔlíwm – water hits ringing, the səlxcín spelling for Inchelium, Washington (Nach-el-ium)

nsəlxcín - Okanagan dialect of Interior Salish language group (in-cel-chin)

nslxʷitkʷ – ocean (in-sil-wha-it-kwq)

ntytyix - salmon (in-tee-tee-huh)

nćiʔcn – wolf (en-ze'chen)

nx̌aʔx̌ʔítkʷ – whale/monster (in-ha-he-itkwa)

qʷspíćaʔ - buffalo (kwas-peet-za)

q̓ʷq̓ʷcwíyaʔ - chipmunk (kots-se-we-ah)

q̓sápiʔ – Sinixt version of "once upon a time" designating the beginning of an ancient story (kasapi)

síyaʔ – saskatoon berries (see-ah)

slaqs– mosquito (se-lux)

səlxcín - Sinixt dialect of Interior Salish language group (cel-tsin)

Secwepemc or *sxʷapmx* – the people to the North of the Sinixt. Also known as Shuswap (sh-wep-mek)

spqmix – swans (spek'mik)

snk̓lip - Coyote (sin klip)

sq̓it – rain (skit)

sqʷl'ip - black moss (squil-lip)

skʷnkʷinm – wild potato (sin-sqeenum)

sɫuqin – spear in the head. Its anglicized version – Slocan – gives its name to a valley, river, lakes, towns, etc. (shlu-kayn)

smum iem – the second law of the Sinixt, the law that everything belongs to the women (smum eem)

snx̌ʷntkʷitkʷ– Columbia River (sinh-nayt-kwa)

sník̓ɫćaʔ – elk (sin-ikthl-tsa)

snínaʔ – owl (snee'nah)

spəpelinaʔ – rabbit (spe-pa-lee-na)

spiƛ̓m – bitterroot (speetlum)

styʔíɫćaʔ – caribou (sti-yilh-tsa)

stx̌àɫq – huckleberries (st-halh)

sumíx – a Sinixt person's power source, often an animal (shoo'mk)

sẃaŕak̓xn - frog (swa-ra-kin)

sx̌ʷusm – soapberries, soopalallie (swissum)

sxʷƛ̓iʔ – male mountain goat (si-hw-pti)

tk'imtk'm – wild strawberry (tik-im-tikum)

tule – wetland plant used in making mats, used for shelter among other things (too-li)

tum xúlaʔxʷ - Sinixt homeland. (toom-who-lau)

whuplak'n – the first law of the Sinixt, the law of the land (whup-lock-en)

x̌aʔx̌aʔ - sacred (ha ha)

x̌aʔx̌ʔúlaʔxʷ – rattlesnake (Hah-ah-ooh-lah)

x̌ʷʕʷaylxʷ – fox (why-ay-looh)

GLOSSARY OF ENGLISH TERMS

Aboriginal – is a term used by colonial governments to designate Indigenous People who they recognize politically/legally. The collective noun used in Canada's Constitution Act 1982 and includes the Indian (or First Nations), Inuit and Metis Peoples so legally it has a place at the terminology table.

Colonialism – is the violent displacement, domination and oppression of peoples inhabiting their traditional homelands by imperialistic governments and cultures. Deliberately inflicted epidemics and forceful removal of children from their families were part of this attempted cultural genocide. This violence is a political framework that is responsible for Indigenous Peoples' current experience of systemic poverty, intergenerational trauma, and lack of access to their land, cultures and culturally relevant practices. Colonial governments still rule the vast majority of so-called countries in the Americas.

Cultural appropriation – is the taking of aspects of other people's cultures without their permission – i.e. theft. It is particularly damaging to peoples and cultures who have been colonized and suffer from the ongoing effects of their cultures being violently disrupted. In North America/Turtle Island, this ongoing theft is rampant in the realm of Indigenous spiritual practices and is a significant component of cultural genocide.

Decolonization – is a movement that seeks to bring to light and change the realities of injustice and oppression faced by Indigenous People through the ongoing process of colonization. Decolonization aims to end the current colonial situation in the Americas and to re-establish the land and its governance to its original inhabitants. Decolonization is also an internal process in which individuals, Indigenous and settler, identify the colonial socialization that guides one's behaviour and take control over changing one's behaviour and one's mind. Before settlers can act in solidarity, they must deconstruct the ways they have internalized colonization as an inevitable part of the natural course of history, and act from resistance to this paradigm. This means centralizing Indigenous voices and perspectives, learning to listen, self-reflect and take action.

First Nation – is a term used to identify Indigenous Peoples of Canada who are neither Métis nor Inuit. This term came into common usage in the 1970s to replace the term "Indian" and "Indian band" which many find offensive. First Nations people includes both status and non-status Indians so there's a need to be careful with its usage, especially if in reference to programs that are specifically for status-Indians.

Indian – "Indian" is the legal identity of an Indigenous person who is registered under the Indian Act and a term used to denote North American Indigenous people. It has fallen out of favour with many people but Marilyn James still likes to use Indian to refer to herself and her broader Indigenous community.

Indigenous – is a term used internationally to refer to peoples inhabiting their traditional homelands but who are governed by outsiders in the form of colonial governments. According to the UN Declaration on the Rights of Indigenous Peoples, "there are over 370 million Indigenous people in Africa, the Americas, Asia, Europe and the Pacific. They are among the most impoverished, marginalized and frequently victimized people in the world."

Indigenous resurgence – is a term used to positively define the process that Indigenous Peoples undergo on the road to decolonization. It is a reassertion of Indigenous rights, responsibilities and culture, including Indigenous governance systems.

Rez – colloquial term for referring to a Reservation (US) or Reserve (Canada). The Rez is where Turtle Island's Indigenous people were sequestered when colonial governments took away their lands.

Settler – is term having come into popular usage during the Idle No More Campaign in Canada, to refer to non-indigenous people, communities and governments. The term settler acknowledges that one is not descended from original inhabitants of the landscape one inhabits. Using the term Settler is a way of identifying oneself as a recipient of the benefits of colonization. It holds within it a choice: to align with the reality that our presence can either be a tool in working towards justice, or it can perpetuate the ongoing trauma experienced by Indigenous People through a system that continues to displace people from their traditional land-base, cultural traditions, and communities.

Turtle Island – is a term proposed and used by some indigenous people to refer to North America.

Some of these definitions were modified based on https://www.ictinc.ca/blog/indigenous-peoples-terminology-guidelines-for-usage by Bob Joseph.

BLOOD OF LIFE COLLECTIVE'S BIOGRAPHIES

Marilyn James was the Spokesperson for the Sinixt Nation in the Canadian portion of her people's traditional territory for over 25 years. She continues to be active as an elder in the responsibility of upholding Sinixt protocols and laws in the Sinixt *tum xúlaʔxʷ* under Sinixt *smum iem* law. She holds a Masters of Education from Simon Fraser University and has developed aboriginal curriculum currently being used in four BC School Districts and on the provincial web platform. Marilyn is an accomplished Storyteller in the Sinixt tradition and has told stories to a wide variety of audiences of all ages in schools, at public gatherings and festivals. She continues to unearth traditional stories and her written work has been published in books and anthologies. She is an ardent advocate for human responsibilities towards land and water. She is a mother of three and has eight grandchildren.

Taress Alexis is a Sinixt mother of two young children who has worked as an Aboriginal Education Support Worker and Teaching Consultant in three BC School Districts where she delivered culturally appropriate materials to school-aged children using Storytelling and crafts. She has also been an active Storyteller at the Kootenay Storytelling Festival since 2006 and works with community members in other contexts to enhance cultural sensitivity towards the First Nations Community. She is currently working on expanding her repertoire of original and traditional Sinixt and other First Nation stories for children and general audiences.

Amber Santos is a German, French, Italian, Saulteaux, Metís and Cree descendant who was raised on Sinixt *tum xúlaʔxʷ* where she currently makes her home with the love of her life. She is an artist and educator who is interested in collaborative art-making as a way of feeling part of something bigger, art-making as a spiritual practice and the public space as a place for building collective creativity, dialogue and a culture of inclusion. She is interested in themes of decolonization, landscape relationship and belonging. Her ongoing work in illustration, community mural-making and painting can be found at www.arti2de.com

K.L. Kivi is a queer settler of Finno-Ugric (Mulk, Estonian) heritage who grew up in a refugee family in the land of the Anishinabek People. She has lived in the unceded Sinixt *tum xúlaʔxʷ* since 1990. She works as a writer, activist, peasant and publisher. She is the author of eight books, including *The Inner Green* and *The Town of Nothing* and the editor of *The Purcell Suite.* She has co-ordinated numerous collaborative community-based projects involving writers, visual artists, activists and the public. She runs Maa Press, a publishing company dedicated to "radically and regionally reliable titles about the Columbia Mountains." She seeks to catalyze awareness and civic involvement with the resurgence of the Sinixt People and in the collective work of decolonization. When not fiddling with words, she is present in the mountains, on the water, being entertained by children, or in her garden.

Catherine Fisher is a settler of German and British heritage who has lived in Sinixt territory since 1993. She collaborates with Sinixt elder Marilyn James to produce a radio program, "Sinixt Radio", which has aired on Kootenay Co-op Radio (KCR) since 1999. In 2012 they created a radio documentary about the legacy of colonialism in the Columbia Basin for the National Campus and Community Radio Association's (NCRA/ANREC) "Resonating Reconciliation" project, funded by the Truth and Reconciliation Commission. She is a long-standing board member of KCR and of the NCRA/ANREC. She is also a photographer who is drawn to industrial sites.

Alison Christie is a queer, fifth-generation white settler with ancestral origins in Wales, England, and Scotland. She was raised on the traditional territories of the Haudenosaunee (Iroquois), Ojibway/Chippewa and Anishinabek peoples with little knowledge of their ongoing struggles or history of resistance. Now making home on the unceded traditional territories of the Sinixt, she works toward visioning narratives of culture and landscape through a de-colonial lens, as well as reconnecting with her own stories of origin. Contributing to the written component of the Blood of Life project has been a journey in cultivating deeper relationship to place, Indigenous solidarity, and storytelling as medicine.

Axel McGown is a pragmatic dreamer, a poet, and a white settler of Scottish and English ancestry who calls Sinixt *tum xúla?x^w* home. Axel has always loved storytelling – from being a childhood bookworm to grappling with the messages, characters, and narratives of this project – and loves to learn and connect through listening to stories, and telling their own. When Axel isn't talking about settler-colonialism, or imperfectly practising solidarity with Indigenous Peoples, they are probably writing a poem, playing sweet ukulele tunes, doing art, or staring at the sky.

ARTIST AND WRITER CONTRIBUTOR BIOGRAPHIES

Lori Barkley is a settler born and raised in Stony/Nakoda (Treaty 7) territory in Southern Alberta. She is a political anthropologist, an educator, and an activist. Her research focuses on identity, place, and sense of home relying on narrative and popular discourses, primarily in the media and more recently court-rooms. Her recent work is a seemingly never-ending journey examining aboriginal policy in Canada and educating settlers about our complicated relationship with Indigenous Peoples, focusing on Sinixt as an example of failed policy in Canada and British Columbia.

Amélie Blanchard is a Montrealer who has relocated to Nelson, BC to follow her dreams and become an art therapist. Prior from graduating from the program at the Kutenai Art Therapy Institute, she graduated from Concordia University with a BFA in Design. In addition to her design classes, Amélie followed many drawing, painting and psychology classes and is, up to this day, constantly experimenting and exploring her artist identity as she is growing into her art therapist shoes.

Hannah DeBoer-Smith was told growing up that there were no First Nations here. Her entire narrative of Nelson was that it was a migratory area, or "spiritually" too potent for anyone to live here - now she knows that's not true. In part through this project she is weaving a more complete and honest narrative of this place she calls home. As an artist, she practises in many different mediums - acrylic, wood, textiles, tattoo, sound and for the piece in this book, printmaking and silk-screening. As they say, she has her fingers in many pies.

Devon Ecru grew in the mountains, not so far from the sea. She fell in love with the Sinixt territory during her time living at the edge of the Slocan River, where she began calling the intricate patterns of joy and grief to wind their way out of her paintbrush. Her work is a practice in remembering. The bravery of the ones who dare to re-imagine the world trickles through her as she re-enchants the corners held down below her feet.

Rhoneil Olha Eurchuk-Luhowy is an experimental musician, producer, and artist, as well as a mentor and counsellor. She has released three full-length albums and has toured her work throughout Canada, the United States and Europe. She creates in collaboration with the rhythms of nature and the voices of the invisibles. She strives to create healing work and to integrate the practice of ritual into her process. Rhoneil aims to embody reverence for nature and spirit through her creations. She shares her work through her website invisiblefriends.ca

Fletcher Fitzgibbon is a writer, storyteller, and accountant currently based in traditional Sinixt territory in British Columbia's Slocan Valley. As a writer of fiction, non-fiction, and poetry, Fletcher's work has been published in sources such as the Westender, In Shades Magazine, and the Black Bear Review. As a performer, Fletcher has delivered his unique blend of spoken word and storytelling at venues across the Pacific Northwest, including the Elephant Mountain Literary Festival and Nelson District Arts Council's Artwalk. In 2016, Fletcher was awarded runner-up in the 2016 Kootenay Mountain Culture Fiction Contest for his story "In Silence, You Can Hear". In 2017,

Fletcher received a grant from the Columbia Kootenay Cultural Alliance and Slocan Valley Arts Council to produce a manuscript of his first full-length novel. When he is not writing, Fletcher is creating Microsoft Excel spreadsheets, wearing long johns, or aimlessly following animal tracks in the snow.

Renée Jackson-Harper, B.A. (University of Toronto), M.A. (York University), is a Ph.D. Candidate at York University and a faculty member in the Department of English and Creative Writing at Selkirk College. Her doctoral dissertation examines the work settler narratives do to write (and overwrite) British Columbia's unceded territories. Her poetry, which considers the ethics of dwelling, has been published in various journals including *CV2*, *Prism International*, *Room of One's Own* and *The Trinity Review*. She is grateful to live and work in the territories of the Sinixt, Ktunaxa, Syilx and Secwepemc.

Gabriel Keczán was born in traditional Haudenosaunee/Mohawk territory in Southern Ontario and raised on a fruit and chicken farm in Beamsville with a large family. The name Keczán is Hungarian. His Mother's people are descended from Scottish and English Canadians. He is passionate about the paradoxical concepts of belonging and exile in the context of decolonization. He has been dwelling in *xaʔxáʔ tumxʷulaʔxʷ*, the unceded traditional territory of the Sinixt people since 2002. He lives with his beautiful wife, son, two bonus daughters and their cat in Nelson. He is an artist, writer, registered therapeutic counsellor, and professional art therapist working with individuals, youth and families. He is also a facilitator of the Work That Reconnects as part of the Great Turning. He recognizes First Nations sovereignty, supports ongoing cultural recovery efforts, and respects and celebrates the Indigenous Knowledge of all people of the earth.

Stephanie Kellett is a contemporary illustrative painter of animals and landscapes who is based in the Slocan Valley in BC. Her solo exhibitions include shows at VISAC Gallery in Trail, and Oxygen Arts Centre in Nelson and many of her paintings are found in private residences across the globe. Stephanie has also created murals in the Slocan Valley, for ArtsWells Festival of All Things Art in Wells and for Re-Imagine Street Art Festival in Penticton. Stephanie has been commissioned to create interactive installations at Shambhala Electronic Music Festival and has also illustrated books. Although she received a Diploma in Fine Arts in 2003, and then a subsequent Degree in Art History in 2008, Stephanie is primarily a self-taught painter. Her paintings involve layers of acrylic washes and glazes, illustrative imagery and collage. Her themes focus on spirit of place and a feminist view of nature, and she aims to tell the stories of these places through her art. www.stephkellett.com

Kiala Löytömäki breathes life into the ever-expanding depths of storytelling. the unfolding stories reach through veils between the world(s) to bring forth messages of healing, pain, grief & beauty in darkness. as a writer and a multimedia artist they pull from the void of creativity that stretches through layers of time. their creations are an everlasting moment where past, present and future collide, where the cycles of birth, life, death are constantly turning. these are the reflections of a tender heart as they heal through trauma, survive through mental health challenges & grasp for life-giving connection. this is how kiala remembers—sewing together the pieces of lost magic, lost ancestry, lost connection in an attempt to revive that which was burned, was silenced, was buried, was stolen. this is praise for the ancestors and praise for all who continue to live, doing the hard work of surviving in a culture that wishes to destroy us. kiala uses the mediums of drawing, painting, sculpture, poetry and music to relate to this infinitely unfurling existence.

Moe Lyons is a long-time resident of the Slocan Valley in unceded Sinixt territory. She has a passion for photography and community organizing. For many years she worked as a typesetter and graphic designer, as well as an organizer, for various progressive organizations. She continues to work for social change on a voluntary basis, primarily with the Vallican Whole Community Centre. She proudly identifies as a dyke and a crone.

Stephanie Meitz is a settler living within Sinixt *tum xúlaʔxʷ*. She and her family moved here three years ago from the Coast Salish Territories. She spends her days and nights looking for ways to dismantle the colonial capitalistic patriarchal system. She is a community organizer, educator, and advocate. Her favourite places to be are in the mountains, near any body of water, and in big cities. She has a Bachelor's degree in political science and philosophy from Concordia University and a Master's in Political Science from UBC. Her academic interests include: decolonization, intergenerational trauma, cognitive science, memory, social policy and political governance, women and gender studies, transitional justice, social movements, and civil disobedience. She loves music (especially political hip hop), reading, biking, snowboarding, films, fashion, and tattoos. Her favourite thing to do is hang out with her family- she is the mother of an awesome 8-year-old daughter and married to her best friend.

Serjão Santos has been painting street art and creating paintings on recycled material in his home city of Recife, Brazil and in Canada, since 1999. In Recife, he collaborated with other artists and painted numerous murals on walls of NGOs, schools and on many streets. He began to give graffiti/ street art workshops to youth in 2003. He has participated in over 40 "Mutirões of Graffiti" since 2005, a grassroots community action-group organized by the Rede Resistência Solidária (Network of Resistance and Solidarity). From 2001-2009 Serjão was employed by the Municipal Government of Recife to work as a liaison between the government and street artists' collectives throughout the city. He played a fundamental role in articulating, diffusing and organizing events for street culture as well as facilitating education workshops for local government and the city's residents to learn about graffiti as an art form. In Nelson, Serjão has had local exhibitions and has painted at many festivals and events. Serjão was the visionary behind The Imaginarium, a 5-artist residency at Oxygen Art Centre of spontaneous painting and paintings in alleyways to create dialogue.

Tayler Schenkeveld is a Métis self-taught artist from Winnipeg, Manitoba. She received a bachelor degree in Native Studies and is currently residing in Nelson, BC where she is training to become an art therapist. She is very passionate about Indigenous issues and plans to focus her future therapeutic practice with Indigenous populations.

Samuel Stevenson is a son, a husband, a father. He loves language and patterns and dance. He is a poet, a settler, an art therapist, a teacher, and a student. He was born in Lheidli T'enneh territory and now lives in Sinixt territory in a house made of cedar and stories. He believes that life is made of grief and beauty. He listens.

Chad Thompson grew up on a ranch bordering Kananaskis country in Alberta. At a young age, he learned a great respect for mother earth and was inspired daily by the vast wildlife and beauty of his surroundings. Drawing pride and inspiration from his native *"ancestory,"* he hopes to enlighten people to the beauty and sophistication of First Nations culture and tradition. Never schooled in art, Chad feels he is influenced constantly by his surroundings: "Mother Earth is the greatest teacher." He has been given opportunities to work with experienced artists in the field and has gained extensive knowledge and experience in mural painting, sculpture, graphic and logo design. Chad works mainly in acrylic paints but also indulges in antler, stone, and wood sculpture, jewelry design, artifact reproduction and replicas, hide painting, leather work, fine woodworking and carpentry. This nature enthusiast also spends time in the Kootenays enjoying fly fishing, bird watching, ski touring and paddling. Chad considers his talents god given and gives thanks to the creator for his abilities and also thanks those who have given support and guidance throughout his career.

Tyler Toews has been creating art since he was a child. He has been working as a commercial artist since 2000 with a specialty in large scale murals. With his childhood friend Steven Skolka, they co-founded a business called Canadian Murals in 2002. In 2011, Tyler continued with Canadian Murals as a solo artist. Since its inception Canadian Murals has completed close to 100 pieces for cities, municipalities, and businesses that can be seen across Canada. In 2014 he began commissions for Cabelas retail stores and has completed 50 murals in four Cabelas outlets across the country. His most recent achievement is completing a prominent mural for the new BC Children's Hospital, scheduled to open in 2017. Over years of painting numerous subjects in murals and executing tens of thousands of square feet of painting, Tyler has refined his craft. He is currently focusing his work on a series of fine art oil paintings that explore our relationship with the natural world. Passionate about the outdoors, his artist's eye captures the heart and feeling of each subject painted. Born and raised in British Columbia, Tyler currently works and resides in Nelson BC. CanadianMurals.com

Christie Van der Burg is an artist who lives and works in the Slocan Valley.

Coleman Webb grew up in Vancouver and developed his desire to paint and make things in high school and soon learned to love street art, hip-hop culture and particularly graffiti art. Soon, he began painting on canvas and expressing ideas alternatively, constantly pushing himself to go bigger and do things uniquely. This brought him opportunities to paint murals, commission custom works and practise his techniques. He works in a variety of mediums, from oils to acrylics, spray-paint to wood and other found materials. He has worked collaboratively with many artists on a variety of projects, shown work and painted murals in Canada, the United States, Europe, Asia, Australia and New Zealand. With no formal schooling in the arts, he has learned from a rich fellowship of artists and mentors along the way and has mentored and worked alongside youth on many projects. He has worked with city officials and community groups to come up with creative ideas for public art projects. He lives in Winlaw, B.C. www.colemanwebb.ca

Tannis Wood graduated from the Bachelor of Fine Arts program at TRU in 2006. She is okay at drawing and sometimes painting. She relocated to Sinixt traditional territory a few years ago in order to further her education, which is surprising considering she acts as if she knows everything already. Tannis is excited to be part of a project that records and shares stories that have long inhabited this area.

REFERENCES

Dove, Mourning. Coyote Stories. Lincoln and London: University of Nebraska Press, 1990.

Lowman, Emma Battell and Adam J. Barker. Settler: Identity and Colonialism in 21st Century Canada. Halifax: Fernwood Publishing, 2015.

Maracle, Lee. Memory Serves. Edmonton: NeWest Press, 2015, pg 254.

McKenzie, Mia. Black Girl Dangerous, BDG Press, Incorporated, 2014, pg 60.

FURTHER READINGS AND EXPLORATION:
ABOUT THE SINIXT:

Arnold, Laurie. Bartering with the Bones of Their Dead: The Colville Confederated Tribes and Termination. Seattle: University of Washington Press, 2012.

Pearkes, Eileen Delehanty. The Geography of Memory: Recovering Stories of a Landscape's First People. Nelson: Kutenai House Press, 2002.

Pryce, Paula. Keeping the Lakes Way: Reburial and the Re-creation of a Moral World among an Invisible People. Toronto: University of Toronto Press, 1999.

ABOUT DECOLONIZATION/ (RE)CONCILIATION:

Alfred, Taiaiake. Peace, Power, Righteousness: An Indigenous Manifesto. Toronto: Oxford University Press, 2009.

Anderson, Kim. A Recognition of Being: Reconstructing Native Womanhood. Toronto: Sumach Press, 2000.

Chrystos. Not Vanishing. Vancouver: Press Gang, 1988.

LaRocque, Emma. When the Other is Me. Winnipeg: University of Manitoba Press, 2010.

Lowman, Emma Battell and Barker, A.J. Settler: Identity and Colonialism in 21st Century Canada. Halifax: Fernwood Publishing, 2015.

Maracle, Lee. Memory Serves. Edmonton: NeWest Press, 2015.

Mathur, A., Dewar, J., DeGagne, M. eds. Cultivating Canada: Reconciliation through the Lens of Cultural Diversity. Winnipeg: Aboriginal Healing Foundation, 2011.

Simpson, Leanne, ed. Lighting the Eighth Fire: The Liberation, Resurgence, and Protection of Indigenous Nations. Winnipeg: Arbeiter Ring Publishing, 2008.

UN Declaration on the Rights of Indigenous People, 2007.
Look for other works by these authors as well as the huge body of literature by Indigenous authors.

INDEX

Photograph by Catherine Fisher

MARILYN JAMES

TARESS ALEXIS

NAVA

ROCCO

AXEL McGOWN

AMBER SANTOS

ALISON CHRISTIE

KL KIVI

MARILYN JAMES~ SINIXT WARRIOR

GORD HILL· KWAKWAKA'WAKW·2017

Art by Gord Hill